SPECIAL SERIES, NO. 20   31 JANUARY 1944

GERMAN SKI TRAINING AND TACTICS

PREPARED BY
MILITARY INTELLIGENCE DIVISION
WAR DEPARTMENT

Published by Books Express Publishing
Copyright © Books Express, 2011
ISBN 978-1-780390-82-6

Books Express publications are available from all good retail and online booksellers. For publishing proposals and direct ordering please contact us at: info@books-express.com

MILITARY INTELLIGENCE DIVISION
WAR DEPARTMENT
WASHINGTON 25, D. C., 31 January 1944

SPECIAL SERIES
No. 20
MID 461

NOTICE

1. Publication of *Special Series* is for the purpose of providing officers with reasonably confirmed information from official and other reliable sources.

2. In order to meet the special requirements of certain headquarters, or in order to conserve shipping space, the distribution of any particular issue may be modified from the standard of 150 copies to a division, 30 to a nondivisional group or regiment, 6 to an independent squadron or battalion, and 2 to an independent troop or company. In an infantry division organized according to T/O & E 7 (15 July 1943), redistribution should be effected as follows:

Div Hq	7	Hq	4
Div Hq Co	2	Hq Btry	2
MP Plat	1	Bns (4)	24
Ren Tp	2	TOTAL, DIV ARTY	30
Ord Co	2		
QM Co	2	Regtl Hq	4
Sig Co	2	Regtl Hq Co	2
Engr Bn	6	Serv Co	2
Med Bn	6	Cn Co	2
Div Arty	30	AT Co	2
Inf Regts (3)	90	Bns (3)	18
TOTAL, INF DIV	150	TOTAL, INF REGT	30

3. In addition to *Special Series*, the Military Intelligence Division issues the following monthly publications: *Tactical and Technical Trends, Intelligence Bulletin,* and *Military Reports on the United Nations*. Distribution to AAF units and installations is made by the Assistant Chief of Air Staff, Intelligence. Army Air Forces, and quantities sent to AGF addresses are recommended by the Commanding General, Army Ground Forces. Requests for additional copies of any MID publication should be made through channels.

4. **Every command should circulate available copies among its officers.** Reproduction within the military service is permitted provided that (1) the source is stated, (2) the classification is maintained, and (3) one copy of the publication in which the material is reproduced is forwarded to the **Dissemination Unit, Military Intelligence Division, War Department, Washington 25, D. C.** Comments on this publication and suggestions for future issues may be sent directly to the same address.

PREFACE

This work is an edited translation of a German manual entitled *Tentative Instructions for the Training and Tactics of Ski Troops* (*Vorläufige Richtlinien für Ausbildung und Kampf von Skitruppen*). Like the *Handbook on Winter Warfare* (*Taschenbuch für den Winterkrieg*), which has been published as "German Winter Warfare," *Special Series*, No. 18 (15 December 1943), the ski manual is based on the experiences of the German forces on the Eastern Front and on lessons learned from the Finnish Army.

It will be noted that German infantry regiments and divisions engaged in winter warfare organize their own provisional ski companies and battalions, and that independent ski battalions also are organized by the Army High Command to be employed as GHQ troops (see par. **23**, p. 59). The only German ski units that are organic are in the SS mountain divisions.

There are numerous references in the text to *Training Regulations for Infantry* (*Ausbildungsvorschrift für die Infanterie, H. Dv. 130/2a*), a manual covering many subjects, including close-order drill, employment of light infantry weapons, and minor tactics. It is a manual designed for the training of the squad, the section, the platoon, and the company. The references to this manual in the text have been preserved in order to show the extent to which the German ski units apply and adapt basic infantry technique to the requirements of training and combat on skis.

One of the lessons learned by the German Army in the snows of the Eastern Front is the crucial importance of training ski troops thoroughly and conditioning them for severe weather. In paragraph **23a**, the manual states: "The possibilities for employment of ski troops depend to a high degree on their state of training. The ski unit must be specially trained before it may be committed. The more advanced the training, the harder may be the tasks assigned to the unit." The manual emphasizes that ski units must be able to operate independently, that they must be aggressive in the defensive as well as on the offensive, and that surprise and deception are decisive factors in ski warfare.

Recent evidence on the subject of ski units shows that in 1941–42 the Germans found it necessary to organize special mobile units for patrolling and counterattack. These units, specially trained for winter warfare, were of two types: (1) GHQ shock battalions, originally referred to as *Jagdkommandos* (raiding detachments) and now known as *Jäger* battalions, which are fully motorized except in winter, when they take to skis, and (2) provisional battalions (see par. **28** of this book, p. 79), formed by infantry divisions from their own personnel who have skiing ability. The evidence also indicates that both the GHQ and the provisional ski battalions are not disbanded at the end of winter but are retained as picked units, known as *Divisions-Bataillone* (divisional battalions), upon which a division ordinarily may rely for counterattack.

Only minor deletions have been made in editing. The aim has been to adhere as closely as possible to the original manual, while presenting it in the language and format of War Department publications. For this edition the illustrations in the original manual have been redrawn and, where possible, improved upon.

Anhang 2 zur H.Dv. 1a
Seite 25a lfd. Nr. 19

Vorläufige Richtlinien
für
Ausbildung und Kampf
von Skitruppen

Vom 1. 8. 42

Oberkommando des Heeres
Gen.St. d. H. / Gen. d. Inf.
Nr. 290/42 (II Geb.)

H.Qu. O.K.H.,
den 1. August 1942.

Die „Vorläufigen Richtlinien für Ausbildung und Kampf von Skitruppen" werden genehmigt.

Mit Ausgabe dieser Richtlinien treten die „Richtlinien für die Ausbildung von Skitruppen" vom 9. Dezember 1941 (Vorschrift ohne Nr., Anhang 2 zur H.Dv. 1a, Seite 18, lfd. Nr. 10) außer Kraft.

J. A.:
Halder.

Supplement 2 to Army Manual 1a
Page 25a, Current No. 19

TENTATIVE INSTRUCTIONS FOR THE TRAINING AND TACTICS OF SKI TROOPS

1 August 1942

(Translation of title page of original)

ARMY HIGH COMMAND   Hq. Army High Command,
Army General Staff/Chief of Infantry   1 August 1942.
No. 290/42 (Vol. II)

Tentative Instructions for the Training and Tactics of Ski Troops is hereby authorized.

These instructions supersede *Instructions for the Training of Ski Troops*, dated 9 December 1941 (unnumbered manual, Supplement 2 to Army Manual 1a, page 18, Current No. 10).

By command of:
HALDER

(Translation of verso of title page of original)

FOREWORD [1]

The manual *Tentative Instructions for the Training and Tactics of Ski Troops* is based on the experience gained from organizing, training, and employing ski battalions, raiding detachments, and improvised ski companies on the Eastern Front, as well as on knowledge gained from the Finnish Army. Necessary deviations from infantry training regulations, due to the specialized nature of ski equipment, have been made.

It is assumed that each member of a ski unit will have at least as much skill in skiing as is required in the *Abbreviated Manual on Ski Training*.

The *Handbook on Winter Warfare*, the bulletin *Characteristics of March and Combat in Winter*, and training films are necessary supplements to winter training.

---
[1] Translation of foreword of original.

CONTENTS

	Page
Section I. **INDIVIDUAL TRAINING**	1
1. General	1
2. Basic Drill	1
3. Carrying Weapons and Equipment	5
4. Methods of Dropping and Rising	7
5. Individual Combat Training	8
a. Working Forward on Skis	8
b. Positions and Firing	11
c. Throwing Hand Grenades	16
d. Close Combat	17
6. Training with the Hand Sled	19
a. Loading of Weapons and Equipment	19
b. The Hand Sled in Combat	21
II. **UNIT TRAINING**	23
7. Squad and Platoon as Components of the Company	23
a. Close-Order Formations	23
b. Extended-Order Formations	26
c. Deployment	26
8. Combat Methods	27
a. Leadership	27
b. Characteristics of Combat on Skis	28
c. The Fire Fight	29
d. Squad and Platoon on Security Patrols	30
III. **HEAVY INFANTRY WEAPONS**	33
9. Mobility and Transportation	33
10. Employment and Effectiveness	33
a. Heavy Machine Gun	33
b. Heavy Mortar	34
c. Infantry Howitzer	34
d. Antitank Weapons	35
e. 20-mm Antiaircraft Gun	35
IV. **MARCHES ON SKIS**	36
11. Principles of Training	36
12. Road Reconnaissance	36
13. Preparations for the March	38
14. The Trail-Breaking Detachment	38
a. Mission, Composition, and Equipment	38
b. Function of Leaders	40
c. Breaking Trail	41
d. Marking the Trails	43

CONTENTS

Section IV. MARCHES ON SKIS—Continued.   Page
    15. March Formations... 44
    16. March Security... 44
    17. March Discipline... 45
    18. Rest... 46

V. PATROLS, ASSAULT TROOPS, AND RAIDING PARTIES. 48
    19. Missions... 48
    20. Strength, Composition, and Equipment....................... 48
    21. Suggested Organization of a Raiding Party.................. 50
        a. Typical Organization................................... 50
        b. Total Personnel, Weapons, and Hand Sleds............... 51
        c. Platoon Headquarters................................... 51
        d. First Squad.. 52
        e. Second and Third Squads................................ 52
        f. Heavy Mortar Squad..................................... 52
        g. Engineer Detachment.................................... 52
        h. Ammunition Supply...................................... 53
            (1) *Total supply*..................................... 53
            (2) *Individual supply for each weapon*............... 53
        i. Miscellaneous Equipment................................ 53
            (1) *Carried on person*............................... 53
            (2) *Carried in rucksack*............................. 53
        j. Medical Equipment...................................... 54
            (1) *Dressings*....................................... 54
            (2) *Medicines*....................................... 54
    22. Employment of a Raiding Party.............................. 54
        a. General Combat Principles.............................. 54
        b. The Approach March..................................... 55
        c. Tactics.. 56
        d. Disengaging Actions.................................... 57

VI. SKI COMPANY AND SKI BATTALION............................... 59
    23. Organization and Employment................................ 59
        a. General.. 59
        b. Training Principles.................................... 59
        c. Principles of Command.................................. 61
    24. Operations... 62
        a. Reconnaissance and Security............................ 62
        b. Attack... 63
        c. Pursuit.. 65
        d. Defense.. 66
        e. Withdrawal from Action................................. 67
        f. Support and Cooperation................................ 67
        g. Cooperation with Infantry on Foot...................... 69
    25. Special Operations... 70
        a. Actions behind Enemy Lines............................. 70
        b. Combat against Guerrillas and Special Units............ 71

CONTENTS

	Page
Section VI. SKI COMPANY AND SKI BATTALION—Continued.	
26. Supply	72
a. Means of Supply	72
b. Supply Dumps	72
Appendix A. ORGANIZATION: SKI COMPANY AND BATTALION	74
27. Organization of the Ski Company	74
a. General	74
(1) *Two-battalion regiment*	74
(2) *Three-battalion regiment*	75
b. Peculiarities of Organization	75
c. Arms and Ammunition	77
d. Clothing and Equipment	77
(1) *Clothing*	77
(2) *Bivouac equipment*	77
(3) *Medical equipment*	78
(4) *Ski and sled equipment*	78
(a) *Ski equipment*	78
(b) *Snowshoes*	78
(c) *Hand sleds*	78
(d) *Horse-drawn sleds*	78
28. Organization of the Ski Battalion	79
a. General	79
b. Peculiarities of Organization	79
(1) *Battalion headquarters*	79
(2) *Headquarters company*	80
(3) *Heavy weapons company*	80
Appendix B. TOWING, SNOWSHOEING, AND DOG TEAMS	83
29. Towing Skiers	83
a. General	83
b. Methods of Towing	83
30. Snowshoeing	85
31. Dog Teams	86
Appendix C. MAINTENANCE OF SKIS AND SLEDS	89
32. Care of Ski and Sled Equipment	89
a. General	89
b. Treatment of Ski Surfaces	89
c. Waxing	89
d. Storing	90
e. Repairing	91
f. Binding	91
g. Ski Poles	92
h. Ski Climbers	92
i. Care of the Sled	92

CONTENTS

Appendix C. MAINTENANCE OF SKIS AND SLEDS—Continued.   Page
- 33. Transportation of Skis 93
  - a. Ski Bundle 93
  - b. Sliding Ski Bundle 94

Appendix D. MEANS OF EVACUATING WOUNDED 96
- 34. General 96
- 35. Hand Sleds and Improvised Means 96

Appendix E. IDENTIFICATION 100
- 36. Individual and Unit Identification 100
  - a. Brassards 100
  - b. Manner of Wearing Belt 100
  - c. Ground Flags and Signals 101
  - d. Passwords and Blinker Signals 101

ILLUSTRATIONS

Figure
1. Position of ATTENTION 2
2. Position of ORDER SKIS 3
3. Position of LEFT SHOULDER SKIS 4
4. Double sling for rifle 6
5. Method of rising to rush 8
6. Advancing by sliding 9
7. Advancing in a crouching position 9
8. Trailing skis while advancing on foot 10
9. Dragging skis while crawling 11
10. Prone firing position, with ski poles used as a rifle rest 12
11. Prone firing position, with ski poles used as an elbow rest 12
12. Kneeling position 13
13. Kneeling position, with ski poles used as a rifle rest 14
14. Pole loops crossed to make a rifle support 14
15. Standing position, with the ski pole used as a rifle support 15
16. Snowshoe used as a base for the bipod of the light machine gun 15
17. Throwing the hand grenade while advancing 16
18. Throwing the hand grenade from the kneeling position 17
19. Throwing the hand grenade from the prone position 18
20. Methods of pulling hand sleds 20
21. Firing from the hand sled, or weapons akja, while advancing 22
22. Squad in line 24
23. Platoon-front formation 25
24. Squad with two hand sleds in skirmish order 27
25. Security tracks around a position near the enemy 31
26. Organization of a trail-breaking detail 39
27. Trail-breaking detachment in formation 41
28. Ambush position on a ridge 58
29. Organization of the ski company 76

CONTENTS

Figure	Page
30. Organization of the ski battalion	81
31. Skiers being towed by horses	84
32. Skiers being towed by a motor vehicle	84
33. Method of strapping the snowshoe	86
34. Methods of harnessing dog teams	87
35. Driver breaking trail for dogs	87
36. Men and dogs hauling a sled	88
37. Method of strapping skis for storage	90
38. Method of mending a broken ski tip	91
39. Method of making a ski bundle	94
40. Sliding ski bundle	95
41. Methods of evacuating the wounded	97
42. Fireman's carry	99

Section I. INDIVIDUAL TRAINING

1. GENERAL

The employment of ski troops in Russia makes it necessary for both officers and enlisted men to acclimate themselves carefully to the weather prevailing there, and to make a systematic adjustment to winter living and fighting conditions. The type of training, from the very beginning, must be keyed to these conditions. A methodically conducted winter-conditioning program, made gradually rigorous, heightens self-confidence and gives the troops, even in winter warfare, a sense of superiority. The object of the training is to enable the troops not only to maintain their fighting capabilities in winter, but also to turn winter conditions craftily to their own advantage. Ski training must be synchronized with combat training. Skiing is only a means of locomotion on the battlefield and should by no means constitute a training aim in itself. Furthermore, all officers and noncommissioned officers must counteract the danger that the discipline of the troops will slacken, that they will lose smartness, and that their formations will become ragged as a result of engaging in skiing activities.

2. BASIC DRILL

The position of attention with skis on is assumed at the command ATTENTION (*Stillgestanden!*). The posture in this position will be the same as prescribed in *Training Regulations for Infantry*. The soldier stands on his skis, which are placed parallel, with the tips flush. The arms hang naturally, the hands holding the pole handles at the loops and resting against the thighs. The poles are held parallel, their rings touching the snow to the rear (fig. 1).

In the position of attention with skis off (ORDER SKIS) the skis, strapped together, are held vertically with the tips up, at the right side (fig. 2). With the right hand, grasp the front edges of the skis at the binding. Both poles are held together

Figure 1.—Position of ATTENTION.

by their handles with the left hand, and their points are placed to the rear, with the rings touching the snow. The left arm is extended downward slightly, with the left hand against the thigh. (When they are strapped together, the running surfaces of the skis are placed against each other. One leather strap is placed below the upturns and another at the heels of the skis.)

If, under exceptional circumstances, the position of attention is ordered while the skis are being carried with the poles strapped to them, the left arm and hand are held as prescribed for the soldier without arms. The points of the poles must not extend beyond the ski tips.

At the command LEFT SHOULDER SKIS (*Ski aufnehmen!*) the poles are thrust with the left hand into the snow, one pace forward (fig. 3). The skis are then placed on the left shoulder,

INDIVIDUAL TRAINING 3

Figure 2.—Position of ORDER SKIS.

sloping backward, and they are grasped at the heels with the left hand. (The movement must be executed carefully to avoid striking the slung rifle.) The poles are then brought to the right side of the body, thrust upright into the snow, and held with the right hand.

The manner of holding the skis while marching is left to the convenience of the individual soldier, but he may not shift the skis from shoulder to shoulder except on command. However, if the command AT EASE (*Rührt Euch!*) is given, the skis may be shifted without command and may be carried on either shoulder in any convenient manner. The ski poles may be carried on the free shoulder and swung behind the head to cross under the skis in order to help bear their weight.

Figure 3.—Position of LEFT SHOULDER SKIS.

With the skis on the shoulder, the position of attention with skis off is assumed at the command ORDER SKIS (*Ski abnehmen!*). The soldier plants the poles in the snow in front of him, grasps the skis at the bindings with his free hand, and takes them off his shoulder. The left hand also is used in bringing the skis down. The movements in placing the skis on the shoulder and taking them down are not executed in unison.

The skis are placed on the feet at the command MOUNT SKIS (*Ski anschnallen!*). The soldier places the skis next to him on the snow, loosens the straps. and arranges the binding. (On a slope he places the skis above him at a right angle to the slope.) Then he steps into and fastens the bindings, rises, and grasps the poles with each hand through the loops. (On a slope the downhill ski is fastened first.)

At the command DISMOUNT SKIS (*Ski abschnallen!*) the soldier loosens the bindings and steps off the skis. The poles are laid alongside the skis in such a way that the loops are next to the bindings. At the command SKIS IN HAND (*Skier in die Hand!*) the snow is removed from the skis, which are then strapped together. The soldier grasps the poles, assumes the position of attention with skis off, and stands at ease.

In executing the commands MOUNT SKIS, DISMOUNT SKIS, and SKIS IN HAND snap and silence are required, but not unison of movement.

Facings are executed at ORDER SKIS or LEFT SHOULDER SKIS in accordance with *Training Regulations for Infantry*; when mounted on skis, facings are executed by stepping around, pivoting on the ski heels. The salute when at a halt is rendered by standing at attention and turning the eyes toward the person saluted. The salute while in movement is given by looking directly at the person saluted, but is given when running downhill only if it is safe to do so.

3. CARRYING WEAPONS AND EQUIPMENT

Weapons and equipment must be arranged in such a way that the ski trooper can take long, sliding steps and move his arms freely. The rucksack or the pack must be packed as flat as possible, with most of the weight in the bottom. No hard objects should be carried in the trouser pockets. The manner of carrying weapons depends on the degree of readiness for action required by the situation; changing from one method to another sometimes must be executed quickly and therefore must be practiced. The rifle is generally slung across the back, the barrel pointing upward to the left.

To prevent the rifle from swinging during the march, it may be tied to the side of the pack with an auxiliary strap or carried with a double sling as shown in figure 4. When the double sling is improvised, the auxiliary strap, which leads under the left arm and across the chest, should be arranged to enable adjustment without unslinging the piece. The butt of the rifle must always be kept back so that it will not interfere with the right hand in handling the ski pole.

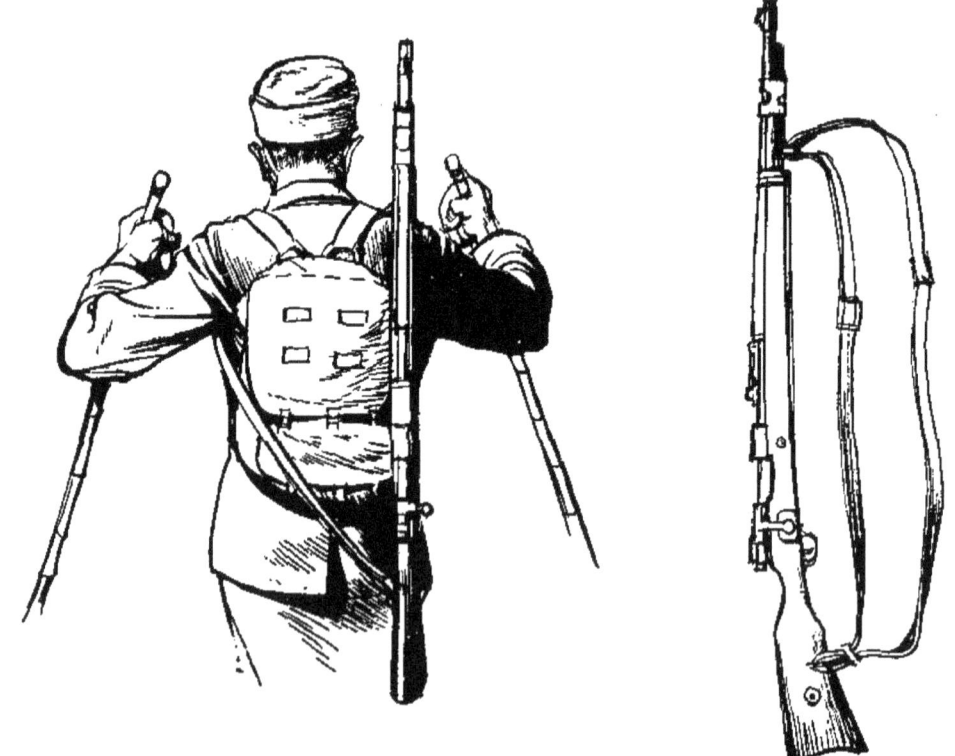

Figure 4.—Double sling for rifle.

In case of an urgent battle alert, the rifle is slung around the neck in front of the body, with the barrel to the right. When in contact with the enemy, the soldier carries the rifle in his right hand, ready for firing; the ski poles are carried in the left hand. The normal methods of carrying, as prescribed in *Training Regulations for Infantry*, are used for the light machine gun, the submachine gun, and the antitank gun, but the methods must be modified to permit free movement of the arms and hands.

Machine-gun ammunition boxes which cannot be transported on hand sleds can be carried best on a packboard, in the rucksack, or strapped to the pack. The light mortar is usually carried on a hand sled or it may be dismantled and carried in the same manner as the ammunition boxes. During marches and in combat, the gas mask is strapped to the lower part of the pack, with the canister cover pointing to the right. When troops are alerted, the gas mask is carried on the chest in such a manner that it will not dangle or get in the way if a man bends down. The bayonet, the bread bag,[1] entrenching tools, and other equipment are carried on the belt, toward the back, where they will not interfere with the handling of the ski poles. The snowshoes are fastened to the pack with straps.

4. METHODS OF DROPPING AND RISING

At the command DOWN (*Hinlegen!*) the man throws himself down in the most convenient manner. He may throw himself prone, with the legs outspread, the tips of the skis pointing outward; or he may throw himself on his right or left side, the skis parallel. It is imperative in dropping that neither weapons nor equipment be damaged, and that snow does not enter the muzzles of weapons. At the command UP (*Auf!*) the soldier rises quickly and stands at ease.

When a man is heavily loaded, he should take great care to avoid falls. Falls with heavy packs waste strength, may render weapons unusable, and frequently lead to injuries. If a soldier cannot avoid falling while running downhill, he should throw himself diagonally backward. When rising, he should place his skis parallel in order to gain a firm position immediately after rising. (On a slope he should place his skis across the slope.)

If in falling the skis get stuck in the snow, or a man sustains physical injuries, it is usually advisable for him to undo the bindings before rising. The troops must be able to strap and unstrap skis quickly, even when lying down. It is every man's duty to assist any soldier who has suffered a hard fall.

---

[1] Similar to the U. S. field bag (musette bag).—EDITOR.

5. INDIVIDUAL COMBAT TRAINING

a. Working Forward on Skis

The manner of advancing and the handling of skis in combat are influenced by the situation, the terrain, and the condition of the snow. When advancing by rushes, the soldier rises from the prone position and supports himself on his left knee. He holds the rifle vertically with the right hand and gives himself additional support by leaning with his left hand on the poles, which are kept together flat on the ground. He then draws up his right foot, sets the right ski in the desired direction, and starts to advance in a crouching position, pushing himself along with the rifle and the poles. (See fig. 5.) While rushing forward, he keeps the rifle in his right hand and the poles in his left. (The method of holding the rifle also applies to the submachine gun, the light machine gun, and the antitank rifle.)

Figure 5.—Method of rising to rush.

When the soldier must slide forward in a prone position, he places his skis close together, lies with his stomach on the bindings, and slides forward by pushing himself with his hands. He may also push with his toes. When this method of advancing is used, the poles are placed on the skis, with the handles under the bindings and the snow rings on the ski tips. The rifle is either slung over the shoulder or laid on the skis in front of the soldier. (See fig. 6.)

Figure 6.—Advancing by sliding.

In deep, loose snow the soldier advances by running in a crouching position. He slings his rifle horizontally in front of him, around his neck. The skis are placed parallel on the ground, separated by the width of his body, and the snow rings of the poles are placed on the skis at the bindings. Bending low and running, he grasps the ski bindings and poles together for support. (See fig. 7.) If the terrain and the combat situation do not permit this

Figure 7.—Advancing in a crouching position.

method of advancing, the soldier goes down on his elbows and knees and pushes himself forward with his knees. The skis he moves forward one at a time, alternately, with his hands. If the condition of the snow is bad, the skis may be trailed while the soldier walks or rushes. He carries the rifle with the right hand, and with the left trails the skis, which are placed on top of each other. The poles may be carried in any convenient manner. (See fig. 8.)

Figure 8.—Trailing skis while advancing on foot.

Skis may be dragged while crawling, or even when advancing by other methods, by means of a cord which is put through the holes in the ski tips and fastened to the belt (fig. 9).

Figure 9.—Dragging skis while crawling.

b. Positions and Firing

Usually only small units, such as patrols and raiding parties, will go into combat with their skis on. When snow and terrain are unfavorable, even small units take off their skis and fight on foot or on snowshoes. A sudden encounter with the enemy, however, may temporarily require even a large unit to engage in a fire fight before the skis can be removed. The *Training Regulations for Infantry* will serve as a general guide for the selection of an individual firing position, and for the conduct of a soldier with skis on while in a given position. In snow-covered terrain, camouflage against aerial and ground observation requires special care. By pressing his body into the snow, the rifleman can conceal himself effectively. The protection against hostile fire which is afforded by cover constructed with snow should not be overestimated. (See the *Handbook on Winter Warfare (Taschenbuch für den Winterkrieg)*.[2])

The various firing positions assumed by troops on skis depend on the terrain and the depth of the snow. Weapons will be handled as prescribed in pertinent weapons manuals, except where contrary directions are given in this manual. Raising the muzzle slightly whenever the weapon is moved in the firing position will prevent snow from entering the unprotected barrel. Care must be taken to avoid the loss of ammunition and other small objects in the snow.

---

[2] Translated and published as "German Winter Warfare," *Special Series*, No. 18 (15 Dec 1943).—EDITOR.

In assuming the prone position, the soldier lies down toward the front with his legs outspread, the tips of the skis pointing outward. The rucksack, the snowshoes, or the crossed ski poles can serve as a rifle rest. When ski poles are used, the pole handles are pushed deeply into the snow and the points are crossed through the snow rings (fig. 10). The poles may also be placed horizontally on the snow to serve as an elbow rest (fig. 11). When the skis are removed from the feet, they may be used for the same purpose.

Figure 10.—Prone firing position, with ski poles used as a rifle rest.

Figure 11.—Prone firing position, with ski poles used as an elbow rest.

In the kneeling position the left ski is placed half a pace forward. The soldier kneels on the right ski, the tip of which is pointed outward at an angle of approximately 45 degrees, and supports the rifle by placing his left arm on his left knee (fig. 12). It is easier to assume this position if the left ski is somewhat higher than the right one. If the bindings have a strong down pull, the kneeling position can be assumed only by placing the right ski to the rear. The rifleman lowers his right leg so that the

Figure 12.—Kneeling position.

foot and ankle lie on the snow and the ski is turned up on edge. The crossed poles, held firmly together by the loops, constitute a rifle rest which is suitable for all variations of the kneeling position. (See figs. 13 and 14.) The poles must be solidly placed in the snow.

In the standing position, the right ski is tilted about 45 degrees outward and the left ski advanced half a pace (fig. 15). The poles remain hanging from the wrist by the loops, but the left one is planted vertically into the snow and, supporting the left hand, serves as a rifle rest.

For firing from the prone position with the light machine gun, the snowshoe is the most practical base for the bipod (fig. 16). The bipod will be firmer if the legs of the bipod are fastened tightly to the binding of the snowshoe. Thus the snowshoe will remain fastened to the bipod on the march as well as in combat. Other improvised rests, such as the rucksack and pine branches, may also be used, depending on the situation.

Figure 13.—Kneeling position, with ski poles used as a rifle rest.

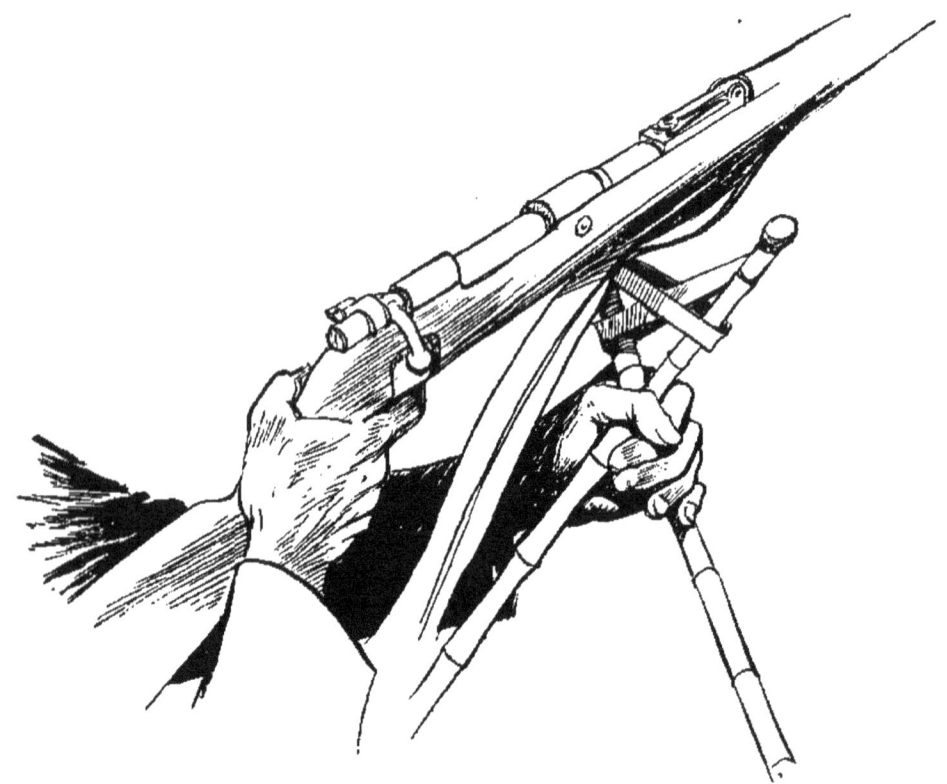

Figure 14.—Pole loops crossed to make a rifle support.

INDIVIDUAL TRAINING 15

Figure 15.—Standing position, with the ski pole used as a rifle support.

Figure 16.—Snowshoe used as a base for the bipod of the light machine gun.

c. Throwing Hand Grenades

When hand grenades are thrown while advancing, the grenade is brought out with the throwing hand while the ski opposite the throwing hand is advanced in the direction of the throw. (See fig. 17.) When drawing the hand back for the throw, the ski on the same side is turned outward approximately 45 degrees. The grenade may be thrown overhand or underhand, with the arm outstretched. The ski which was placed sideways is to be brought back to its former position at the same time. The rifle is held with the free hand during the throw; the poles hang by their loops from the wrist of the free hand.

Figure 17.—Throwing the hand grenade while advancing.

When hand grenades are thrown while kneeling, the left (right) ski is advanced in the direction of the throw. At the same time, the man goes down on his right (left) knee and brings back his right (left) hand for the throw. (See fig. 18.)

INDIVIDUAL TRAINING

17

Figure 18.—Throwing the hand grenade from the kneeling position.

When the snow cover is thin or frozen hard, the right (left) ski may also be turned up on edge and pushed backward to the right (left). In this way, the man can assume the kneeling position shown in figure 13, page 14.

Throwing hand grenades from the prone position requires great skill and special practice. After the rifle and poles have been laid aside, both skis are placed parallel on the ground to the right (left). Without changing the position of the skis, the soldier, with bent knees, pulls the right (left) hand back for the throw and pushes himself forcefully up from the ground with the left (right) hand, which rests on the poles. The hand grenade is then thrown overhand, the momentum of the body being utilized in the movement. (See fig. 19.)

d. Close Combat

In close combat the mobility of a man on skis is limited. Therefore, the skis are usually taken off before engaging in close fighting. They will be brought forward later by men designated for the purpose so that they will be readily available for continuing the attack or for pursuit.

Figure 19.—Throwing the hand grenade from the prone position.

To exploit favorable momentary situations, however, it may sometimes be advisable to engage in close combat on skis. For this purpose, the poles are slipped under the belt to free the hands for handling weapons. Sometimes the poles themselves may be used as weapons.

Since the fragmentation of the hand grenade is reduced in deep snow, hand grenades are successful only if they are thrown with careful aim. The potato-masher type of grenade is preferable to the egg-shaped grenade because it does not roll away on the snow. The heavy winter clothing of the rifleman, gloves, and the difficulty of finding a solid position for the feet may decrease the throwing range considerably.

INDIVIDUAL TRAINING 19

The methods prescribed in *Training Regulations for Infantry* will be followed basically in firing the light machine gun and the submachine gun while walking on skis. Skiing ability and much practice are required.

6. TRAINING WITH THE HAND SLED

a. Loading of Weapons and Equipment

Light and heavy infantry weapons, ammunition, rations, and bivouac and other equipment, which are too bulky or too heavy to be carried by the man, are loaded on hand sleds when troops are committed.

The most suitable type of hand sled is the akja.[3] It is used in two forms: the boat akja and the weapons akja. The boat akja is used to carry ammunition and equipment. When lined with blankets, it may also be used for the transportation of casualties. In the weapons akja, the weapon is mounted and fired from the sled. The light and heavy machine guns, the light mortar, and the antitank rifle are the weapons most suitable for mounting on sleds. The weapons akja is open at the back to facilitate the handling of the weapon from the prone position. In place of the boat and weapons akjas, other types of hand sleds, improvised by the troops themselves, may be used. (See the *Handbook on Winter Warfare*.)[4]

When the combat situation makes it necessary for the squads and platoons to take hand sleds along, they are loaded either before the march or during a long rest period while on the march. Weapons akjas are loaded by the crews of the weapons.

If early contact with the enemy is not expected, weapons and ammunition should be wrapped in shelter halves and tied to the sleds to protect them against snow and moisture during long marches. Hauling of the sleds is made easier if the heaviest part of the load rests on the back part of the sled. If possible, the

---

[3] Finnish *ahkio*, literally "Laplander's sled."—EDITOR.

[4] See "German Winter Warfare," *Special Series*, No. 18 (15 Dec 1943), par. 65, p. 197.—EDITOR.

load should not exceed 60 kilograms (132 pounds). If the situation requires a higher degree of alertness, weapons and ammunition should be stowed so that they can be taken off the sled and used instantly. Weapons which can be fired from the sleds should be kept loaded and ready to fire.

The hand sleds are pulled by means of towropes, which are placed over the chest or shoulder, or around the waist of the skier. Two skiers are usually required to haul a loaded hand sled. When snow conditions are very good, the sled can be pulled by one man for short distances.

As a rule, the triple-track method is used in pulling a hand sled. In making such a track the last man keeps only one ski in one of the tracks of the man in front of him. With his other ski he cuts a third track.[5] If the sled is pulled by more than two men, they walk in a formation which is most likely to improve the track for the sled. The towropes should be of different lengths so that the men do not get in one another's way (fig. 20).

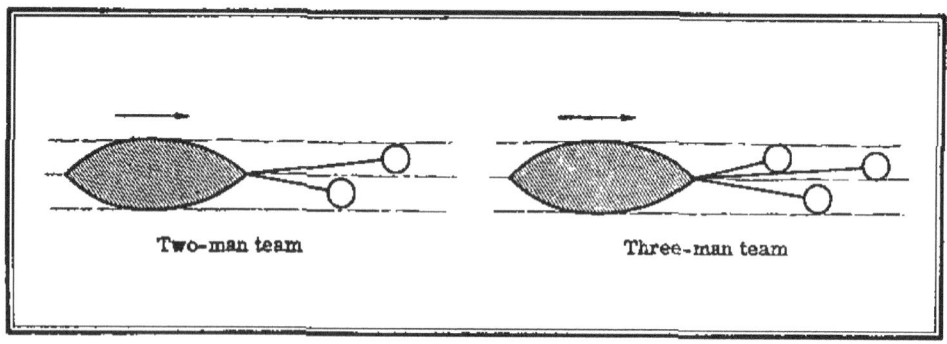

Figure 20.—Methods of pulling hand sleds.

When negotiating obstacles, hollows, and sharp curves, it is advisable to assign a skier to help control the sled from the rear by means of a brake rope attached to the back of the sled. In difficult places he can help the pulling crew by pushing the sled with the ski pole. The packs of the towing teams should be as

---

[5] See "German Winter Warfare," *Special Series*, No. 18 (15 Dec 1943), par. 10b, p. 31.—EDITOR.

light as possible. When going uphill or when hauling in very slippery snow, the sled pullers should use ski climbers. At times it may be necessary to substitute snowshoes for skis. The squad or platoon leader sees to it that the towing crews are relieved regularly.

When sled dogs and proper harness are available, the hand sled can be hauled by a dog team, but the weight of the load should not exceed the aggregate weight of the dogs. Near the enemy, only well-trained and obedient dogs may be used. Even so there is the danger that the dogs may betray their presence by barking and thereby make a surprise advance of the unit impossible. (For details concerning dog teams, see appendix B, par. **31**, p. 86.)

b. The Hand Sled in Combat

Because of its low silhouette and its easy mobility in every kind of snow-covered terrain, the hand sled can be used everywhere on the battlefield. Its employment depends on the tactical requirements of the situation and of the terrain.

When fire is to be delivered from the weapons akja, the sled is pulled into position and advantage is taken of all possible cover. The gunner lies down in the akja, bracing his feet against the snow in order to hold the sled in place while firing. If necessary, twigs, brushwood, or similar materials are placed under the sled or the sled is held firm by another man.

If sudden contact with the enemy occurs during a march or during deployment, the immediate use of the weapon on the weapons akja must be assured even while advancing. The man detailed to fire the weapon follows the sled in order to be able to take position and fire at once. The hauling crew steps out of the field of fire and takes cover.

During an advance or change of position under enemy fire, the hand sled is pulled forward by bounds by the hauling crew, who advance by crouching or sliding. In weapons akjas mounted with a light machine gun it may be advisable, if snow and terrain permit, for Gunner No. 1 to remain in the prone position in the akja in order to be able to fire the weapon while the sled is in motion (fig. 21).

Maneuvering the hand sled on the battlefield, taking firing positions on the weapons akja, and advancing with this vehicle require considerable practice before they can be mastered by the pulling and gun crews.

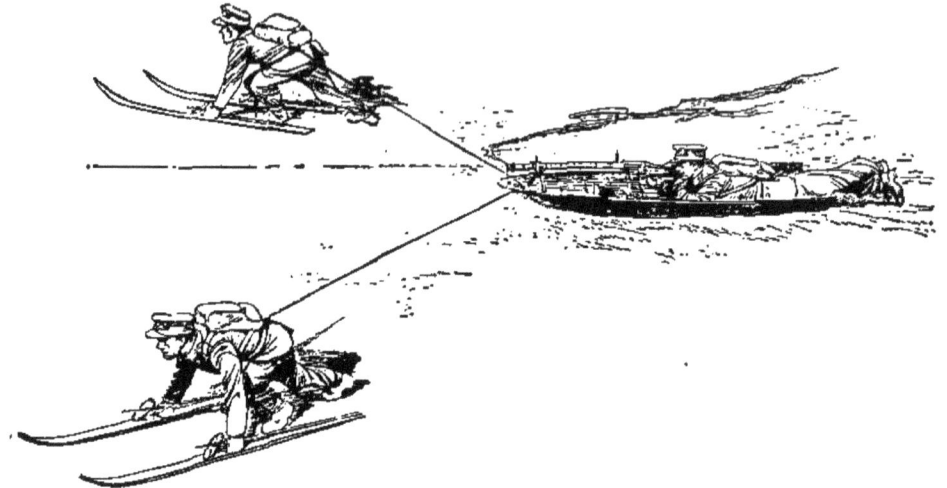

Figure 21.—Firing from the hand sled, or weapons akja, while advancing.

Section II. UNIT TRAINING

7. SQUAD AND PLATOON AS COMPONENTS OF THE COMPANY

a. Close-Order Formations

Close-order formations are used by ski troops on marches and in movements on the battlefield. (There will be no close-order drill on skis or with hand sleds.) Before falling in, the soldier will sling the rifle and other weapons. Close-order formations of ski troops mounted on, or carrying, their skis will be executed as prescribed in *Training Regulations for Infantry*. The only exceptions are that commands of execution for troops mounted on skis must be given slowly and drawn out, and that hand signals are given with a ski pole. On the battlefield, signals with the pole will be used exclusively.

The organization, equipment, and missions of the ski squad are, in general, as prescribed in *Training Regulations for Infantry*, but it is advisable to increase the number of men to 11, in addition to the squad leader,[1] in order to reinforce the towing crews of hand sleds. It is also desirable to equip the squad with at least 1 rifle with a telescopic sight, 1 grenade discharger (for rifle grenades), and 2 semiautomatic rifles. Because the usefulness of the light mortar is reduced in snow, it can, in most instances, be dispensed with by the platoon. Besides the squad leader, the second-in-command should also be equipped with a submachine gun. Changes in strength, composition, and equipment of the squad may be ordered to meet the requirements of the situation.

When the squad falls in, the weapons akja is placed 1 pace behind and between Gunner No. 2 and Gunner No. 3 (towing crew)

---

[1] The German basic infantry squad normally includes a squad leader and 9 men, but specialized infantry squads may number as few as 7 and as many as 16. See "The German Squad in Combat," *Special Series*, No. 9 (25 Jan 1943), par. 1, p. 1.—EDITOR.

(fig. 22).² In column formation it is placed behind Gunner No. 3. The towing ropes are held ready for pulling by the sled detail. Intervals in close-order formation are 2 paces between men; intervals between ranks, 1½ ski-lengths.

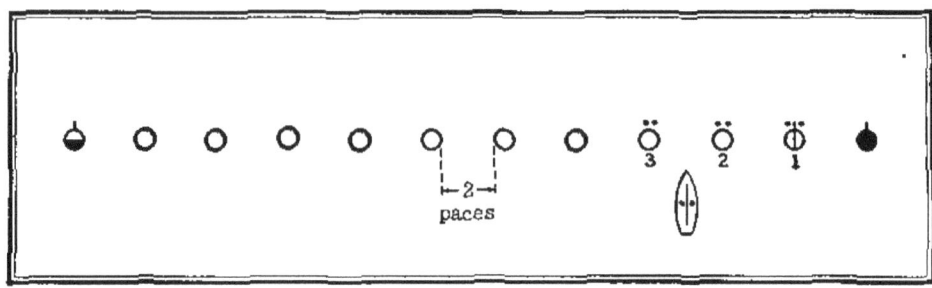

Figure 22.—Squad in line. (For a key to the German symbols, see note 2, below.)

Because the strength of the squad is increased to 12 men, including the squad leader, the platoon is reduced to 3 squads. It is advisable to substitute a third runner for the bugler.

In the platoon-front formation, squads are aligned at intervals of 1½ ski-lengths between ranks, with platoon headquarters on the left flank of the leading squad. The normal marching formation is obtained by facing the squads to the right, with platoon headquarters marching as file closers. If a light mortar squad is attached, it falls in at the left flank of the platoon-front formation or in the rear of the platoon in squad-column formation, in accordance with *Training Regulations for Infantry*. (See fig. 23.)

Any additional sleds for ammunition, rations, or bivouac equipment will be placed on the left flank of the platoon-front formation or in the rear of the units in platoon column.

---

² The following is a key to the German symbols used in figs. 22, 23, 24, and 27.—EDITOR.

Platoon leader   Squad leader   Assistant squad leader   Leader, platoon headquarters   Light machine gunner No. 1

Light machine gunner No. 2 or 3   Rifleman   Runner   Litter bearer   Weapons akja   Boat akja

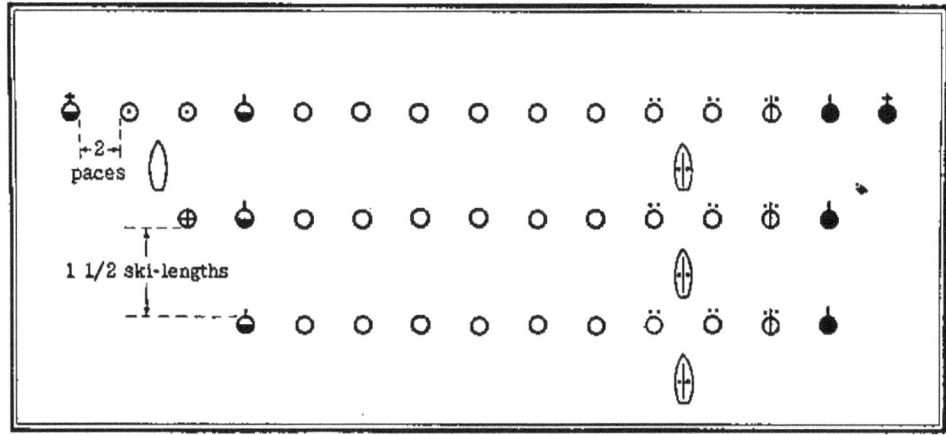

Figure 23.—Platoon-front formation. (For a key to the German symbols, see p. 24, note 2.)

To form a single file from a squad in line, at the command 1. FORM A SINGLE FILE FROM THE RIGHT, 2. MARCH (*Reihe rechts—Marsch!*), the right guide marches straight forward. After he has reached a distance of 1½ ski-lengths, the other men follow at the same interval.

When forming a column of files, the leaders of the second and third squads march at right oblique so that they can fall in behind the last man of their respective squads at intervals of 1½ ski-lengths. Platoon headquarters moves into the file at the rear of the first squad; the light mortar squad and the litter bearers march in the rear of the third squad.

To march the squad forward from column formation, at the command 1. SQUAD (SECTION), 2. MARCH (*Gruppe (Abteilung)—Marsch!*), the first man steps off and the men behind him follow at intervals of 1½ ski-lengths.

At the command HALT (*Halt!*) the first man comes to a halt and stands at ease; the others close up, halt, and stand at ease. If possible, halts should be made on level ground. The men who draw the sled march in file so that they do not hinder one another. The machine gunners, if they are not needed to tow the sled, follow behind the weapons akja.

If track conditions are bad, the squad leader may order his akja to the rear of the squad, in which position it will have the advantage of a trail packed by the entire squad. Thus the work of the towing crews is made easier. This practice will normally be necessary for the leading squad. Reliefs for the men pulling sleds are ordered by the squad or platoon leader when the platoon marches as a unit.

b. Extended-Order Formations

Extended-order formations for ski troops are substantially the same as those prescribed in *Training Regulations for Infantry*. When the men are mounted on skis, the extended squad column is the normal formation. It is formed from the file by increasing the intervals. Because of the difficulty of breaking separate tracks, men in line of skirmishers have to exert themselves considerably. Consequently this formation should be employed only when the intention is to open fire.

When the squad is deployed as a line of skirmishers, contact with the weapons akja must be maintained (fig. 24). Hand sleds (boat akjas), which are used for hauling equipment only, follow in the rear of the squad. The interval to be maintained is ordered by the squad leader.

c. Deployment

Deployment is executed, in general, according to the directions contained in *Training Regulations for Infantry*. Some variations may be necessary because of the difficulties of executing movements quickly and flexibly in deep snow and off broken trails.

The considerable marching depth of the platoon in single file impairs readiness for action. Therefore, when approaching the enemy, deployment on a broad front takes place earlier than when marching without skis. In order to take advantage of the terrain, however, and in order to reduce the number of tracks, the squad should remain in file as long as possible.

As a rule, the platoon leader, with platoon headquarters, follows behind the leading squad. He may temporarily go to the point of the platoon for reconnaissance purposes, or he may move freely to the various points along the route which afford observation.

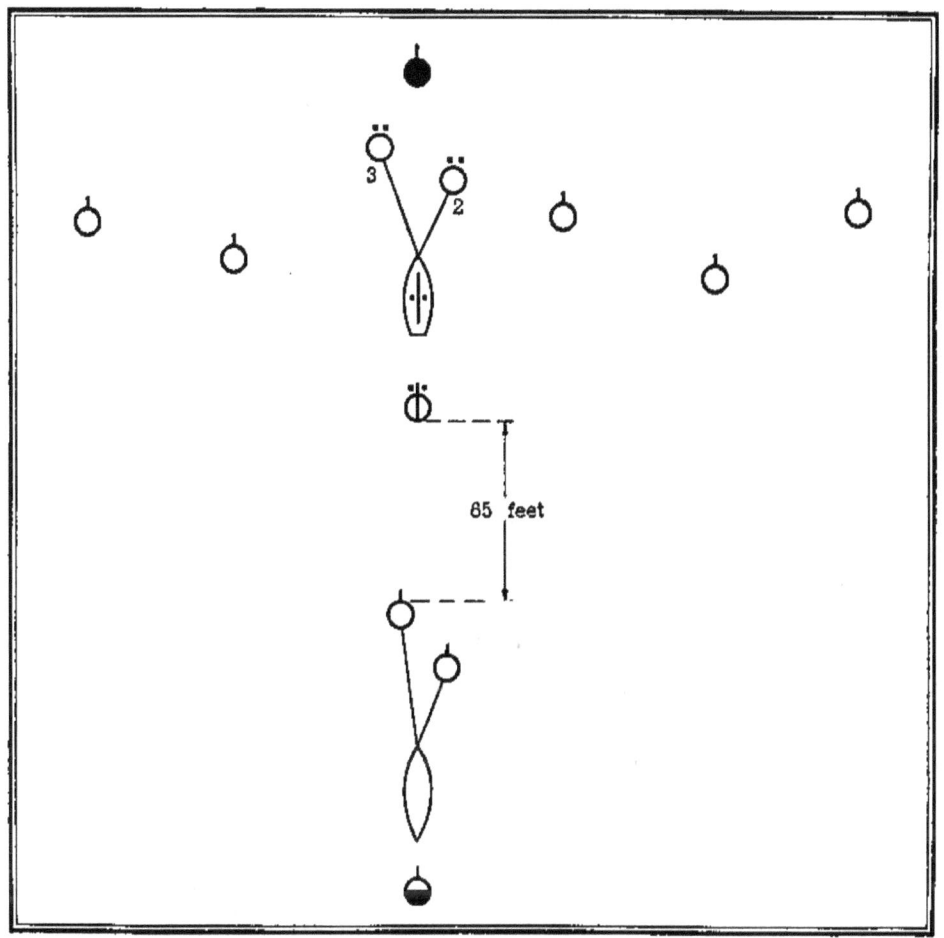

Figure 24.—Squad with two hand sleds in skirmish order. (For a key to the German symbols, see p. 24, note 2.)

8. COMBAT METHODS

a. Leadership

The squad or platoon leader must have great physical strength and initiative. He must frequently depend entirely on his own judgment when the main body of his unit is distant and his personal example has a decisive influence upon the conduct of the men. Poor skiers and soldiers not familiar with winter conditions are not suited as squad leaders of ski units.

The peculiarities of the employment of ski troops require that the squad or platoon leader have special aptitude as a leader of scouting patrols, raiding parties, and other such independent missions. He must be specially trained, therefore, in orientation in open terrain and in carrying out marches on skis.

He must also be familiar with the employment of, and cooperation with, heavy weapons units, with the handling and care of weapons and equipment in snow and cold, with the duties of engineer troops, and particularly with the construction of improvised shelters. Knowledge of first aid for wounds and frostbite, as well as protection against cold, is required of every subordinate leader.

b. Characteristics of Combat on Skis

In combat on skis, the swift execution of all movements on the battlefield and the ability to deceive and outwit the enemy in every situation play a great part and greatly increase the striking power of even small units.

Squads and platoons frequently are specially organized and reinforced with heavy weapons and signal and engineer equipment to enable them to accomplish missions independently. Care must be taken that the mobility of the unit is not thereby impaired. Pieces of equipment which might reduce speed must be left behind or deposited during the approach march at selected points on the terrain.

When approaching the enemy, advantage should be taken of poor visibility, such as fog, snow squalls, twilight, and darkness. Creeping skillfully and without a sound toward the enemy is of decisive importance in gaining a quick and thorough success. Close contact must be maintained within the squad and platoon. It is the responsibility of every unit to keep contact not only with the units to the right and to the front, but also with those to the left and to the rear.

During attack and pursuit, envelopment should always be sought by utilizing mobility. Only weak forces should be left in front to deceive and pin down the enemy. It may be practical temporarily to detach the light machine gun of one squad operating on the flanks and employ it frontally.

If an attack bogs down in snowy terrain shortly before the objective is reached, heavy casualties usually result. Therefore, a decision must be sought as soon as possible and with the greatest tenacity. In choosing the direction of an attack, consideration must be given to the fact that difficult skiing terrain frequently offers better possibilities for a surprise breakthrough than favorable skiing terrain.

Close combat is usually decided by the use of small arms and grenades. If possible, close combat should be started with a surprise attack; if on skis, by a rapid downhill run. It may be more practical in certain instances to avoid meeting the enemy in hand-to-hand combat and to seek a decision through a fire fight within the most effective range.

By equipping troops with skis it is possible to conduct a mobile and aggressive defense. Ski troops must be utilized to a particularly great extent against an enemy who is not equipped with skis and whose mobility is limited.

c. The Fire Fight

Fire fights of the infantry in snow-covered terrain take on added importance because the terrain can be kept under observation more easily and also because visibility is usually better. In cases where ski troops have no artillery support, fire fights alone are frequently the only means of securing the success of the engagement.

Increasing the allotment of telescopic sights to riflemen strengthens the fire power of the squad and favors the more frequent firing of single shots. Concentration of the fire of all rifles with telescopic sights to overpower important single targets (enemy leaders, observation posts, and machine guns) can be of particular advantage before and during an attack, and also in defense. Because of the limitations of transportation in ski warfare the platoon or squad leader must control the use of ammunition.

Snow and extreme cold can materially influence the conduct of the fire fight. In particular, it should be borne in mind that in extreme cold, small arms cannot be touched with bare hands; gloves or mittens should be worn. This necessity affects the rate of fire and accuracy. Low temperatures also affect the rate of fire and accuracy. Weapons at first fire somewhat short, but after a few rounds will function normally. Distances appear deceptively short in snow-covered terrain which has a completely white background. Cartridges and parts of weapons must not be placed directly in the snow but must be protected from moisture. The depression caused in the snow and the blackening of snow by muzzle blast in front of a weapon give away the location of the gunner and force him to change his position frequently.

d. Squad and Platoon on Security Patrols

Ski troops frequently fight alone, independent of larger units. Such tactics require special security measures and increased watchfulness on the part of all troop employed as security patrols. At night and with poor visibility, in terrain which is difficult to observe and is near the enemy, all normal security measures must be increased. As a matter of principle, at least two men should always be assigned to patrol and sentry duty. The leader charged with maintaining security will decide whether sentries and patrols shall move on skis or on foot. Sentries at fixed posts must be camouflaged day and night.

Long hours of guard duty in any weather, particularly after strenuous marches, are part of the training of every ski unit and must also be required of all members of supply columns. Constant supervision and care of sentries and patrols is one of the most important tasks of the squad or platoon leader assigned to security duty.

To provide immediate security for quarters located near the enemy, a circular ski track may be made. This is established, depending on the situation and the terrain, at a radius of about 1,000 or 1,500 meters (1,094 to 1,640 yards) around the position, in a manner permitting observation of enemy terrain. The track, however, should be concealed as much as possible. (See fig. 25.) Outposts or sentries are established in heated tents, sheds, or farmhouses at the roadside or other points important for the protection of the position. Old tracks, extending beyond the security circle, should either be properly marked or be obliterated. Patrols and runners should cross the security circle only on previously designated and marked tracks. Patrols from the outposts guard the security track by constantly circulating on it. Branches placed

UNIT TRAINING

across the track serve as a means of checking whether the enemy has used it.

If new tracks of unknown origin are discovered, patrols will investigate and, if necessary, alert the outposts. A second narrower track may be constructed around the quarters and guarded in a similar manner to provide close-in protection.

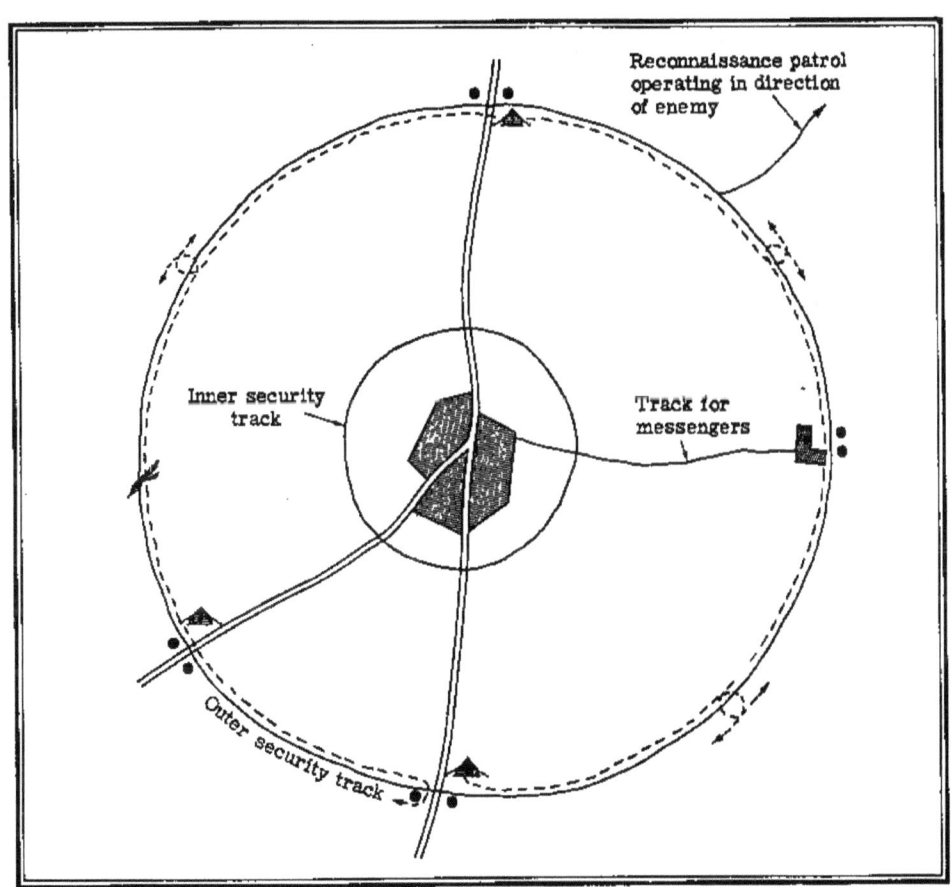

Figure 25.—Security tracks around a position near the enemy.

Tracks for messengers must permit speedy skiing, and it must be possible to find them without difficulty even in the dark and in foggy weather. Snow squalls require frequent renewal of the tracks. In extreme cold, special trails for ski or foot travel should be prepared in the immediate vicinity of the sentries to give them an opportunity to warm up by vigorous movements. Sentries should be relieved at short intervals.

To increase security and to protect sentries and outposts, various simple obstacles and alarms should be constructed on tracks or communication roads leading toward the enemy. Trip wires hidden in the snow and connected with mines, booby traps, or alarm mechanisms are particularly useful.

Listening posts are especially important at night in snow-covered terrain, and also in daytime, if the position is defiladed. At night, patrols, sentries, and outposts should be equipped with flare pistols and an ample supply of flares. Regardless of the protection provided by circular ski tracks, reconnaissance by scouting patrols in the direction of the enemy cannot be dispensed with.

Section III. HEAVY INFANTRY WEAPONS

9. MOBILITY AND TRANSPORTATION

The employment of heavy infantry weapons in a ski unit depends generally on the means of transportation available and the degree of mobility which is possible. Heavy weapons must be mobile to such an extent that they can follow the ski unit even off trails and roads. A few mobile heavy weapons with much ammunition are generally more useful than many weapons which lack mobility.

Hand sleds are the best means of transportation for heavy weapons that can be dismantled, such as heavy machine guns, heavy mortars, antitank rifles, light mountain infantry howitzers, and 20-mm antiaircraft (*2-cm Flak*) guns. The ammunition for these weapons should also be loaded on hand sleds.

Weapons of great weight which cannot be dismantled are loaded on runners or special sleds and are hauled by horses or tracked vehicles. The special sleds must be of the same gauge as standard horse sleds. They should have a low silhouette and it should be possible to fire the weapon from the sled.

When advancing cross-country, it is generally possible to carry heavy weapons and their ammunition supply on horse sleds or runners, but only on previously prepared tracks.

10. EMPLOYMENT AND EFFECTIVENESS

a. Heavy Machine Gun

The fundamentals of the employment of the heavy machine gun remain essentially unchanged. Observation of the cone of fire, preparation of the position, and adjustment fire in snow-covered terrain require special training. The weapon is usually fired from the hand sled. Employment from a camouflaged position will be possible only in exceptional cases. Firing over our own troops is permitted only if the gun mount is resting on a firm base

In difficult and defiladed terrain it may often become necessary to carry the heavy machine gun without its mount and use it as a light machine gun. It is advisable to fire a number of single rounds before beginning automatic fire in order to warm up the barrel and the breech mechanism.

b. Heavy Mortar

The heavy mortar is the most important high-angle weapon of the ski company. Carried on hand sleds, it can be transported with relative ease. Adjustment fire usually requires a larger amount of ammunition than is needed under normal conditions. In low temperatures the weapon at first fires somewhat short; therefore, adjustment fire should be started at a greater range than that originally calculated. Fragmentation of mortar ammunition decreases in deep snow. A correspondingly higher expenditure of ammunition is therefore to be expected. If the snow is thin or frozen over, mortar shell 38 (*Wgr. 38*)[1] is particularly effective.

Mortar shells must be cleared of snow before they are inserted in the barrel. It is advisable to leave the tube brush in the barrel until shortly before firing so that particles of snow and ice will be removed when the brush is withdrawn.

c. Infantry Howitzer

Selection and preparation of the firing position for the light mountain infantry howitzer require increased care during the winter. The best effect is obtained by ricochet fire, which can be used on frozen ground and in loose snow up to a depth of 16 inches. On hard frozen ground, the guns or the runners on which guns are mounted should, if possible, be placed on a support such as brush, fascines, or rush mats. In deep snow, guns must be prevented from sinking in by placing them on broad supports. Care must be taken to find soft ground for the spades. Because of its great weight, the heavy infantry howitzer can be employed by ski troops only in rare cases.

---

[1] An air-burst shell.—EDITOR.

d. Antitank Weapons

In equipping ski troops with antitank weapons, the antitank rifle 41 (*Panzerbüchse 41*) is the likeliest choice. When dismantled, it can be transported on hand sleds and is therefore suitable for the support of smaller units on raiding parties, scouting patrols, flank security units and similar independent missions.

The 37-mm antitank gun (*3.7-cm Pak*), when pulled by troops, can be transported only for short distances and when off the road can be moved only over prepared tracks. Horses or motor vehicles must be used to haul it for long distances. Therefore, its use by ski troops is limited. Unmotorized antitank weapons of larger calibers are usually not suitable for use by ski troops.

The principles of employment of antitank weapons remain essentially unchanged. Fire from position should not be too close to the top of the snow; otherwise the snow will be blackened by the first shot. To prevent snow from swirling in front of the muzzle, a snow camouflage cloak or similar cover should be placed beneath the barrel.

e. 20-mm Antiaircraft Gun

The single-barreled model (*Einling*) of the 20–mm antiaircraft gun (*2-cm Flak*) can be used by ski troops, but because of its great weight, the gun can be transported off the road only when dismantled. The four-barreled model (*Vierling*) is not suitable for use by ski troops. The firing position should be chosen to permit fire against both aircraft and ground forces. In preparing the position and employing this weapon, the principles laid down for the heavy infantry howitzer and the heavy antitank weapons may be applied. The sliding parts require particular care during the winter. For adjustment of the weapon, rounds should be fired singly before changing to automatic fire. Quick assembly and disassembly of the weapon in snow must be practiced.

Section IV. MARCHES ON SKIS

11. PRINCIPLES OF TRAINING

Training for marches on skis is an essential part of the training program of a ski unit. The training must build the man up to a point where he can enter combat after a long march, fully able to fight. Starting with a light pack, the load of the troops should be gradually increased until full field equipment is carried. The speed and the distance of the marches, as well as the time spent in skiing over difficult terrain, should be similarly increased.

The rate of march over long distances should be as uniform as possible. The skiers should get warm without perspiring. Under normal snow and weather conditions a ski unit without horse-drawn sleds can march 50 percent faster than infantry on foot. A heavy snow storm, however, especially from the direction of march, decreases the rate considerably.

Systematic adjustment to bad weather and low temperatures are as important as learning to ski skillfully. In extreme cold it may be advisable to alternate marching on skis and marching on foot; for example, about 2 miles on skis, and about a half-mile on foot. In deep snow, however, marching on foot is normally possible only on prepared trails and hard-packed paths; otherwise snowshoes must be used.

12. ROAD RECONNAISSANCE

In winter, road and terrain conditions are subject to constant changes due to climatic influences. Systematic reconnaissance of the march route, planned in advance, is therefore indispensable, even in a difficult position. It must be carried out with all available means, including aerial photography and interrogation of the civilian population and of neighboring troop units, even if reliable maps are available. If the situation and nearness of the enemy do not permit sending a separate reconnaissance unit ahead, adequately reinforced scouting or trail-breaking details carry out road reconnaissance. These details must always be dispatched early enough to obtain important information before the march is begun.

In the selection of the route of march, it must be remembered that frozen rivers, brooks, lakes, and swamps frequently offer the easiest and therefore the quickest means of approach for ski troops. These frozen bodies of water must be thoroughly tested for their carrying capacity.

The extent of the reconnaissance mission is dependent on whether the march is to be carried out with skis and hand sleds or whether horse sleds are also to be used. When horse sleds are in the column, more time must be allowed, for the reconnaissance will usually have to be more thorough.

In general, the reconnaissance mission covers the following points:

a. Condition of existing trails and roads.
b. Depth and type of snow.
c. Gradients.
d. Possibilities for by-passing points under enemy observation, obstacles, and bad stretches of the route.
e. Carrying capacity of ice.
f. Measures to be taken to negotiate difficult places (requirements in man power, material, and time).
g. Wind-protected resting places and possibilities for emergency shelters.

The composition and equipment of the reconnaissance details depend on the difficulties which are expected. Small obstacles must be removed by each detail without specific order. It is usually advisable to attach engineers.

It may frequently be necessary to send out several reconnaissance patrols in different directions in order to select the most suitable route of march. It is important to remember that a detour may frequently lead more quickly to the objective than a shorter but worse route. Only skilled skiers are detailed for reconnaissance duty. Patrol leaders must possess sufficient experience to select routes for ski troops. Commissioned officers must be given command of large or important patrols.

13. PREPARATIONS FOR THE MARCH

Preparations for the march are based on the results of reconnaissance. They depend on the purpose and the duration of the march, the condition of the ground and the weather, the enemy situation, and the composition of the unit. In selecting equipment, it is essential to cut down weight as much as possible. The prevailing situation must be considered in determining the equipment and the total load which may be carried.

The equipment must be checked, if possible, on the day preceding the march. The check should cover, above all, the condition of the skis, the poles, the bindings, the ski climbers, and the spare parts. In regard to horse and hand sleds, it must be ascertained whether the loads are properly distributed and securely fastened, whether the harness and towropes are intact, and whether the sleds themselves are in good order.

The weapons, especially the machine guns, must be thoroughly cleaned and the grease removed, and, if it is snowing, must be protected with covers.

The uniform must not hamper the movements of the skier. If the clothing is too warm, it induces perspiration, which might cause colds during halts. In extreme cold or strong winds, an application of antifrost salve is advisable before leaving the shelter. If possible, fresh socks and underwear should be put on before the beginning of a long march. An extra, dry change of socks and underwear should always be carried in the pack.

The men must have sufficient sleep before strenuous marching. Enough time must be allowed to enable the troops to eat a substantial hot meal before beginning the march.

14. THE TRAIL-BREAKING DETACHMENT

a. Missions, Composition, and Equipment

Every unit must be thoroughly trained in trail-breaking and must practice it in any weather, at any time of day, and in all conditions of snow. A trail-breaking detachment is formed only if the unit is of platoon strength or larger, and is employed to break trails in deep, soft, and trackless snow in order to facilitate the advance of its parent unit. If the situation does not permit the employment of such a detachment, the unit must break its own trail. In easy terrain and under normal conditions, the trail may also be cut by road reconnaissance units.

The trail-breaking detachment is divided into several trail-breaking details, the number of which depends on the number of tracks to be cut. One trail-breaking detail is designated as the guiding detail and the others follow in echelon. A trail-breaking detail usually consists of a leader and 6 to 10 men (fig. 26).

Personnel	Special equipment	Duties
Lead man (80-foot interval)	Wire cutters	Cuts the first tracks.
Direction observer (30-foot interval)	Compass, binoculars, and hatchet.	Directs the lead man by compass.
Trail improver (15-foot interval)	Brush knife	Improves curves.
Squad leader (15-foot interval)	Compass, map, and binoculars.	Selects the route; controls speed; provides security; relieves the lead man.
Two trail improvers (Variable interval, depending on the situation)	Hatchet and spade	Pack and finish the trail; provide security.
Two trail markers (Variable interval, depending on the situation)	Brush knife, spade, and trail-marking equipment.	Mark trail and provide security.
Relief man		

Figure 26.—Organization of a trail-breaking detail.

The trail-breaking detachment of a company will normally consist of one or two details; that of a battalion, one or two platoons. When snow is heavy and the weather is bad, the detachment must be doubled. The number of tracks to be made depends on the composition of the column, as well as on the strength and composition of the unit which follows. Ski tracks can be used for horse-drawn sleds, or special sled trails may be cut.

The lead which the detachment must have depends on the situation, the condition of the snow, and the weather. In general, it will be about one-half hour for each 3 miles. The detachment, in addition to cutting tracks, removes small obstacles, employing wire cutters, hatchets, brush knives, spades, and other tools. Its personnel must carry only minimum loads.

When operating in the vicinity of the enemy, the trail-breaking detachment also provides security for the parent unit. It must be ready for defensive action, even if reconnaissance patrols have been sent ahead. Reinforcement of the detachment with light machine-gun crews and riflemen may be advisable.

b. Function of Leaders

The leader of the trail-breaking detachment is to be instructed in his duties personally by the commander of the parent unit. The mission must include definite instructions concerning the route (its azimuth should be given on a map, or it should be pointed out in the terrain), the number and type of required trails, the time of departure of the trail-breaking detachment and of the main unit, the objective, the intended rest areas, and the measures to be taken when meeting the enemy and after the mission has been accomplished. Furthermore, the leader is to be informed of the intelligence and reconnaissance measures taken in connection with the execution of his mission.

The leader of the trail-breaking detachment organizes the column, designates the guiding detail, specifies the azimuth, the intervals between the details and their special equipment, and the positions of himself and his assistant.

The guiding detail cuts the main trail and is usually in the middle of the formation. (See fig. 27.) If the route follows roads, railroads, and deep cuts, a different detail may be assigned the guide functions. If the detachment has hand sleds, they usually follow in the main trail behind the reserve detail. The leader of the detachment, as a matter of principle, remains with the guiding detail, accompanied by one or two messengers. He does not participate in the actual work of breaking trail.

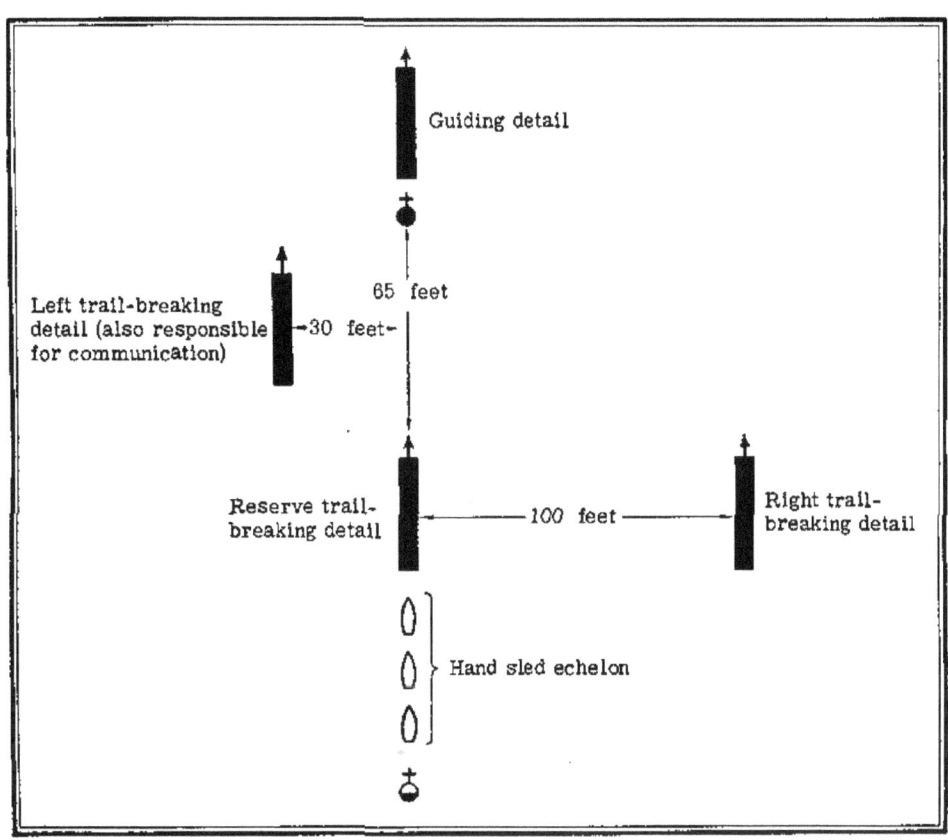

Figure 27.—Trail-breaking detachment in formation. (For a key to the German symbols, see p. 24, note 2.)

c. Breaking Trail

A trail should be broken out in as simple a manner as the terrain permits. The requirements of the unit which follows and not the convenience of those who are cutting the trail are the important factors. Since even minor obstacles can retard the march considerably, they should be by-passed as often as possible. It must be remembered that uphill tracks become more slippery as they are used. Brush, straw, or similar materials should be placed over wet spots so that the troops can pass over them without getting their skis wet. If obstacles cannot be by-passed, several sets of tracks must be broken out over them so that units which follow can cross on a broad front.

To save energy, uphill tracks should have as few turns as possible. Slopes should be uniform and adapted to the poorest skier.

On curves, skis are not to be raised off the ground. They must be slid on the snow into the desired direction. If the ski tracks are too narrow, they soon become useless. An 8-inch width is suitable for most skiers.

Unless special tracks must be prepared for horse-drawn sleds, one or several horse-drawn sleds can be attached to trail-breaking detachments for breaking a trail. They follow in the main trail 65 to 100 feet behind the last detail. When several sleds are used, they should carry varying loads, the heaviest sleds being assigned to the rear of the column.

For short distances, a usable path for horse-drawn sleds can be made by packing the snow. This may be done most effectively by a detail on snowshoes. When large units are marching, it is advisable to break out a separate trail for line-of-communication traffic. It is advisable to lay it directly alongside the main trail.

Snowfalls obliterate tracks within a short time. It then becomes necessary to send the trail-breaking detachment ahead with only a slight start or to send a second detachment to renew the trail just before beginning the ski march.

The mileage covered by the trail-breaking detachment depends on the terrain and character of the snow. Under normal conditions, the detachment can break the trail for a day's march of a larger ski unit. To maintain endurance and to guarantee an uninterrupted march, the leading men of the trail-breaking details must be regularly relieved. In very deep and heavy snow, a relief may become necessary every 300 feet. When the change is ordered, the man to be relieved steps sideways out of the tracks and falls in at the end of the column, while the man following him becomes the point. Special equipment is exchanged. In a well-trained ski unit the soldiers assigned as leading men relieve one another even without specific orders. Under difficult conditions it may be advisable to relieve the whole guide detail from time to time with a reserve detail.

The work of the trail-breaking detail is supervised by its leader. He gives the necessary instructions for improving and finishing the trail. At particularly difficult places, he may take over the point for a short time and break trail himself.

d. Marking the Trails

Each trail-breaking detachment should mark its trail as uniformly as possible. The type of markings to be used must be known to the unit that follows. When several details are operating, the marking of the trail cut by the guiding detail is usually sufficient. The marking should be simple, but recognizable by night as well as by day. For tracks in new snow which will be used only once or only temporarily, it is sufficient, where other tracks or roads are crossed, to erect unobtrusive markers. Trails which are intended for frequent use over a long period must be marked more permanently.

The following may be used as trail-markers:

(1) Distinct signs in the snow (for instance, three impressions with the snow ring of the ski pole, close together).
(2) Twigs on trees and shrubs broken in a predetermined manner.
(3) Poles or guiding arrows planted in the snow.
(4) Markers made of rags or colored paper.

Snowfalls, fog, and poor observation necessitate especially thorough and frequent trail-marking. Orientation is facilitated if the markers are numbered successively in the direction of march and spaced at uniform intervals.

"Snow men," which can be erected quickly, may be used as effective road markers over wide, flat terrain unbroken by vegetation.[1]

In order to avoid the destruction or obliteration of trail-markers by traffic, the markers should be placed about 3 feet off the trail. When strange tracks cross the trail of the unit, they must be obliterated at the point of crossing. It may frequently be advisable to post sentries at crossings to direct units that follow.

If a section of the route is under enemy observation or can be used only at certain times or under certain conditions (for instance,

---

[1] "'Snow men' have proved to be specially effective. They are constructed of blocks of snow, 39 to 47 inches tall, with an opening at a height of about 31 inches in the direction of march. In the opening is placed a very thin pane of ice, through which refracted rays of light can be seen over relatively great distances even when visibility is poor" ("German Winter Warfare," *Special Series*, No. 18 (15 Dec 1943), par. 9, p. 29).—EDITOR.

with great intervals between men, or without horse-drawn sleds), a sign must be erected at a suitable spot in front of the vulnerable section of the route with the necessary information, such as "Enemy observation within 300 feet; passable only after dark." The prompt removal of all trail-markers after the route has been used must be enforced.

15. MARCH FORMATIONS

Single file is the usual march formation of the ski unit. In order to shorten the depth of the file, which is four to six times the depth of a unit marching on foot, platoons should, whenever possible, march in several parallel sets of tracks. Companies and larger units will always do this, and their sections with horse-drawn sleds will march as close together as possible on a single trail.

When advancing into battle, the march formation will be determined exclusively on the basis of tactical considerations. The formation of a march column on a large scale requires detailed orders. This is particularly important when marching in heavy snow and bad weather as well as in darkness and cloudy weather. The relief of units marching at the head of the column is necessary from time to time.

If sufficient engineer forces are not already with the reconnaissance squads, engineers should be incorporated into the head of the column, adequately equipped with tools for the removal of obstacles. At the end of each column, reserve skis as well as spare parts and repair tools must be carried on hand sleds, if possible. If packed roads are available, horse-drawn sleds may use them while the skiers march on several sets of tracks on the adjoining open terrain. Skiers must be detailed to protect each sled echelon that is marching independently and to aid the sled crews at difficult places.

16. MARCH SECURITY

The security measures prescribed in *Training Regulations for Infantry* will serve basically also for the security of a unit marching on skis. Units detailed for other purposes (breaking trails, reconnaissance) also share in security tasks.

Snow and cold carry noises over long distances. Therefore, any unnecessary noise must be avoided during the march. For each column and each squad on the march, certain skiers should be detailed to stop frequently at the side of the road to listen for noises indicating enemy activity. Flank and rear guards should be kept as mobile as possible and should be equipped only with the absolute minimum of hand sleds. When visibility is good, they advance in bounds from one point of observation to another. When difficult terrain and bad weather interfere with the maintenance of a secure system of communication by means of messengers on skis, it may be necessary to equip security units with radio equipment.

On the approach of enemy aircraft, the skiers leave the trail and disperse, taking cover by crouching and supporting themselves with their arms on the skis. They remain motionless in this position until the all-clear. The skis, unless they are painted white, must be covered quickly with snow. Horse-drawn sleds remain on the trail and the drivers stay with the horses. All riflemen and machine-gun crews take part in the defense against low-flying air attack. To deceive enemy air observers, it may be advisable to employ a special detail to obliterate the tracks left behind by the column. This precaution is especially important when entering woods and villages and when leaving billets.

17. MARCH DISCIPLINE

The regulations concerning march discipline in *Training Regulations for Infantry* apply generally also to the march of a ski unit. The marked route must be followed in accordance with the requirements of track discipline. Leaders of all grades must strive to maintain continuity of the march even under adverse climatic conditions and to eliminate delays as soon as possible and by all available means.

The march pace must not be allowed to slacken on slight uphill slopes, and the troops must not bunch up at the start or finish of a downhill stretch but must continue the march at the normal pace. Obstacles must be negotiated on the broadest possible front without slackening the speed of the march.

Troops marching close to horse-drawn and hand sleds will promptly help to push sleds over obstacles without waiting for orders. When crossing frozen bodies of water whose carrying capacity for loaded, horse-drawn sleds seems doubtful, the horses are unhitched and the sleds unloaded; troops will then haul the sleds across the ice surface. Units in the rear must be warned of difficult sections of the road which require special attention. This can be done by erecting suitably worded signs, by passing back a message from man to man, or by posting a sentry.

It is advisable to halt briefly after crossing a large obstacle in order to close up the column and to check for stragglers. In every unit on the march, one man (if possible, an officer or noncommissioned officer) should be detailed as end man to supervise march discipline. If a man must fall out, he immediately clears the tracks by stepping aside and reports to the end man, who tells him how to continue the march. If the man will be delayed for a long period, a second man must always be detailed to accompany him. The same procedure is followed when sleds fall behind.

18. REST

After about three-quarters of an hour of marching, a short halt of from 5 to 10 minutes is ordered for straightening out ski bindings, hand sleds, and clothing. During such a halt the skis remain on the feet and the sleds stay in the trail. The frequency of rest periods depends on the situation, the snow, the weather, the availability of suitable resting places, and the degree of fatigue of the troops. Unless it is planned to eat, the rest should not last longer than 20 minutes.

In extreme cold and biting wind, efforts should be made to accomplish the march without rest. Under such conditions, rest periods do no good and easily cause colds. Villages, woods, underbrush, and depressions sheltered from the wind, which offer sufficient concealment against ground and air observation and can easily be guarded, are the most suitable rest sites. If possible, water should be nearby and resting places should be selected some distance from the track. If the rest is to last several hours, the possibility of ordering a bivouac must be considered. Units should be directed to the resting site by means of signs or sentries.

The skis are taken off during a rest period only when the leader of the unit orders it. When the temperature is below freezing and the skis are removed, they must be placed on the snow with the running surfaces down. During a thaw, the skis should be planted in the snow, tips down, and snow must be kept off the running surfaces. If necessary, skis may be rewaxed during long stops.

To prevent colds, underclothing wet with perspiration should be changed during a rest stop and dry clothing put on. During a long rest, warm drinks should be issued. Snow must not be used to quench thirst. All tracks made during a rest must be obliterated as effectively as possible, in order to avoid giving clues to enemy air and ground reconnaissance. The march is resumed at a moderate pace which is accelerated gradually to normal marching speed.

Section V. PATROLS, ASSAULT TROOPS, AND RAIDING PARTIES

19. MISSIONS

The ski patrol is the most important reconnaissance organization in snow-covered terrain. It may be employed for combat reconnaissance as well as general reconnaissance. Its missions may sometimes last several days.

Training Regulations for Infantry, in the section entitled "The Squad in Reconnaissance," applies in general to ski patrols. Because of its mobility the ski patrol is particularly fitted to execute, besides reconnaissance, minor combat missions to disturb and harass the enemy. Detachments on skis which are organized for the sole purpose of executing limited combat missions are designated as ski assault troops.

A raiding party is used chiefly for the demolition or destruction of distant objectives or for missions behind enemy lines. It must be able to accomplish combat missions independently, fighting for several days without relying on the supply installations of the main unit. In particular, raiding parties may be employed—

a. To conduct reconnaissance in force over large areas;

b. To destroy enemy artillery positions, to annihilate troops and reserves separated from their units, and to raid command posts;

c. To destroy shelters, supply installations, and transport facilities;

d. To intercept and destroy food or ammunition supply columns and to cut off and interfere with enemy supply and communication lines;

e. To protect wide sectors against enemy guerrillas, paratroops, and airborne troops.

20. STRENGTH, COMPOSITION, AND EQUIPMENT

The strength, composition, and equipment of ski patrols, assault troops, and raiding parties depend to a great extent on the mission, situation, and probable length of separation from the main unit. The guiding factors in selecting personnel for these ski groups are aggressiveness, marksmanship, and proficiency in skiing. Especially versatile officers or noncommissioned officers must be detailed as leaders. The assignment of a man who speaks the language of the enemy or of the local inhabitants is advantageous.

The usual strength of a ski patrol is one squad. For the accomplishment of certain missions, it may be reinforced with engineers and artillery observers. As a rule, hand sleds are taken along only if the mission is to last an entire day. The assignment of a radio team is usually advisable.

The organization and equipment of the ski assault unit are based on the requirements of the mission. The strength of the unit varies between a squad and a platoon.

The strength of a raiding party ranges from a platoon up to a company. As a rule, heavy weapons and antitank weapons are attached. The mobility of the raiding party, however, must not be impaired thereby. Heavy weapons loaded on hand sleds are generally preferable to those which can be moved only on horse-drawn sleds. Assault guns or tanks may be attached to raiding parties.

In selecting equipment to be taken along, the aim must be to achieve the greatest possible economy in weight. The equipment which will permit the individual soldier to maintain his fighting strength must be based on the tactical requirements of the contemplated action. Written orders or maps with overlays which may be of value to the enemy must not be taken along.

Maximum fire power and mobility are decisive factors in determining the type and number of weapons with which the individual ski trooper should be equipped. Therefore, the men must be equipped with the largest possible number of automatic weapons, rifles with telescopic sights, and a correspondingly large supply of ammunition. Half of the total personnel will be equipped with submachine guns and semiautomatic rifles.

The number of heavy weapons to be taken along depends on the facilities for carrying sufficient ammunition. Fewer arms and plenty of ammunition should be the rule. The amount of rations, bivouac, signal and orientation equipment, pioneer and medical supplies, as well as ski repair equipment, depends mainly on the expected duration of the action. Prepared, nourishing foods, rich in fat (which, moreover, do not occupy much space and are not affected by weather conditions) will, if possible, be taken along as rations. Every third man is to be equipped with cooking gear.

Bivouac equipment will always be taken along if bivouacs in the snow, outside villages, are expected. Although tents which retain heat weigh more, they are preferable to those which do not. For actions in terrain without vegetation or inhabitants, fuel must be taken along. In his pack every man carries blankets and warm, windproof, and water-repellent clothing.

Larger patrols and raiding parties will be equipped with a radio of sufficient range for communication with the main unit. This equipment is transported on a hand sled, ready to operate. For purposes of orientation, it is necessary to take along compasses (at least two for each squad), binoculars, watches, and also sufficient material for marking trails (arrows, flags, paint, colored paper, and other articles).

Engineer equipment, such as explosives, concentrated and magnetic charges, and mines, are taken along if the mission may require their use. An abundant number of wire cutters, hatchets, spades, and hand saws is usually advisable. Medical equipment, carried on a hand sled suitable for transporting wounded men, consists mainly of bandages, antifrost materials, and stimulants.

It is indispensable, even for the smallest ski unit, to have ski repair equipment, including spare parts for bindings, spare tips for skis, and the necessary repair tools. For longer missions, it is also necessary to take along extra skis and poles.

21. SUGGESTED ORGANIZATION OF A RAIDING PARTY

a. Typical Organization

A typical organization for a raiding party consists of one platoon, reinforced by one heavy mortar squad and one engineer detachment. It is assumed, for purposes of illustration, that the party will be gone for 2 days.

PATROLS, ASSAULT TROOPS, AND RAIDING PARTIES 51

b. Total Personnel, Weapons, and Hand Sleds

Officers	1
Noncommissioned officers	7
Other enlisted men	58
Rifles	23
Semiautomatic rifles (with telescopic sights)	14
Pistols	13
Submachine guns	16
Light machine guns	3
Heavy mortar	1
Tripod for heavy machine gun	1
Hand sleds	13

c. Platoon Headquarters

Personnel	Weapons and equipment on person
1 officer (leader of raiding party).	1 submachine gun, 1 pair of binoculars, 1 lensatic compass.
1 noncommissioned officer (assistant platoon leader).	1 submachine gun, pair of binoculars, 1 lensatic compass.
4 messengers	1 submachine gun, 1 semiautomatic rifle with telescopic sight, 2 rifles, 1 Very-type pistol with signal ammunition, 2 light hatchets.
1 medical noncommissioned officer.	1 pistol, 1 pair of binoculars, 1 lensatic compass.
2 first-aid men	2 pistols.
2 litter bearers	2 rifles.
Other equipment	1 hand sled with 1 heavy machine-gun tripod (for mounting light machine gun as heavy machine gun), 1,200 rounds of ammunition in belts, 1 spade. 1 hand sled with 2 pairs of spare skis and poles, repair kit, aluminum ski tips, spare bindings, collapsible lanterns, 1 spade, rations. 1 hand sled with medical equipment and reserve ammunition. 1 hand sled for transportation of wounded.

d. First Squad

Personnel	Weapons and equipment on person
1 noncommissioned officer (squad leader).	1 submachine gun, 1 pair of binoculars, 1 lensatic compass.
3 machine gunners	2 pistols, 1 rifle, 1 pair of binoculars, 1 light hatchet.
8 riflemen	1 submachine gun, 3 semiautomatic rifles with telescopic sights, 4 rifles, 3 light hatchets, 1 wire cutter.
Other equipment	1 hand sled with 1 light machine gun (bipod with snowshoe base), 1,200 rounds of ammunition, and 1 spade.

e. Second and Third Squads

The second and third squads are identical with the first squad.

f. Heavy Mortar Squad

Personnel	Weapons and equipment on person
1 noncommissioned officer (squad leader).	1 submachine gun, 1 pair of binoculars, 1 lensatic compass.
1 range setter	1 pistol.
11 men	3 pistols, 4 semiautomatic rifles with telescopic sights, 4 rifles, 4 light hatchets, 1 wire cutter.
Other equipment	1 hand sled with 1 heavy mortar and 2 spades; 4 hand sleds with ammunition (18 rounds for each sled).

g. Engineer Detachment

Personnel	Weapons and equipment on person
1 noncommissioned officer (detachment leader).	1 submachine gun, 1 pair of binoculars, 1 lensatic compass.
5 men	5 submachine guns, 2 light hatchets, 1 wire cutter.
Other equipment	1 hand sled with hand grenades and with explosives and engineer equipment as required by the mission.

h. Ammunition Supply

(1) *Total supply.—*

Rifle (and semiautomatic rifle)	4,400 rounds.[1]
Pistol	416 rounds.
Submachine gun	6,144 rounds.
Light machine gun	4,800 rounds.
Heavy mortar	72 rounds.
Hand grenades	162.
Explosives	As required by the mission.

(2) *Individual supply for each weapon.—*

Rifle (and semiautomatic rifle)	120 rounds (100 on person, 20 on hand sled).
Pistol	32 rounds (on person).
Submachine gun	384 rounds (256 on person in 8 magazines, 128 on hand sled).
Light machine gun	1,600 rounds (1,200 with each light machine gun, 400 with platoon headquarters).
Heavy mortar	72 rounds (on sleds).
Hand grenades	2 for each man (on person), 30 on hand sleds.

i. Miscellaneous Equipment

(1) *Carried on person.—*

Shoes, semiwaterproof and large enough so that 2 or 3 pairs of socks may be worn.
Socks (2 or 3 pairs).
Winter combat suit (quilted trousers, fur-lined jacket, fur cap).
White camouflage suit.
Gloves (1 pair).
Fur-lined leather mittens (1 pair, worn over gloves).
Wristlets and knee protectors.
Woolen underclothing.
Skis and ski poles (1 pair of each).
Sheath knife (1 each).
First-aid packets (2 each).

(2) *Carried in rucksack.—*

Shelter half.
Woolen socks (2 pairs).
Personal cooking and mess equipment.
Newspaper.
Candles and matches.
Rations for 1½ days (additional rations for one-half day on hand sled).
Portable gasoline cook stove (1 for each squad).

---

[1] Issued in the proportion of six rounds of armor-piercing tracer cartridges to one ball cartridge.—EDITOR.

j. Medical Equipment

(1) *Dressings.*—Muslin bandages, medicated compressed gauze pads, elastic bandages, wire ladder splints (additional splints to be improvised, if necessary).

(2) *Medicines.*—Litter bearers' kits, antifrostbite ointments, dextroenergen or pure dextrose, *Pervitin*.

22. EMPLOYMENT OF A RAIDING PARTY

a. General Combat Principles

Skill in outwitting the enemy, courage, and a ruthlessly aggressive spirit are prime requisites for the success of ski patrols, assault units, and raiding parties. Fast action, in which the element of surprise is utilized, secures superiority, even against a far stronger enemy. In a surprise engagement with the enemy, to attack is almost always the right thing to do.

The main principles of combat procedure are—

(1) To get off the roads into the snow, and approach the enemy cross-country.
(2) To get out of the villages and march through woods.
(3) To remain mobile.

If the mission leads behind enemy lines, it is advisable to utilize the night or foggy weather in order to penetrate the outposts of the enemy. Through early reconnaissance it must be determined where openings in the enemy's defenses are located and where his flanks may be by-passed. (See also par. **25a**, p. 70.)

A meeting with numerically superior, equally mobile enemy units must be avoided, if the mission can be accomplished without combat. Envelopment or surprise by the enemy must be prevented by increased watchfulness.

Every commitment demands the exact formulation of an operational plan by the leader. The plan and mission must be known to every member of the ski patrol, assault unit, or raiding party. In general, the plan must cover the following phases of the mission: route of march, main track, conduct if contact is made with the enemy, execution of the specific mission, rendezvous after the mission has been accomplished, return to the main body.

b. The Approach March

The approach march requires careful husbanding of strength in order to enable the unit to reach its objective in good physical condition. The return route will be designated during the approach march and will be marked when necessary.

The march is carried out in accordance with paragraphs **15** to **18**, pages 44 to 46. Ski patrols of squad strength break their own trails. They generally send scouts ahead. Raiding parties send out one of several trail-breaking details, which also provide security during the march. Marching on several parallel sets of tracks reduces the depth of the column and at the same time increases preparedness for combat. To save strength, it may be advantageous, in certain areas, to tow ski patrols and raiding parties behind horses or motor vehicles. (See appendix B, par. **29**, p. 83.)

Tracks of unknown origin must be treated with the greatest suspicion. They may have been prepared by the enemy and may be mined or may lead to an ambush. Small detachments may prevent accurate estimation of their strength by the enemy by ordering all men to insert their poles in the same places as the preceding men, or by keeping their poles raised in certain areas. Consequently the enemy will be unable to make an accurate count of the pole marks in the snow.

The manner of carrying the weapons depends on the degree of readiness for combat which is necessary, and will be ordered by the unit commander.

The approach is made by bounds from observation point to observation point, using covered routes. If it is necessary to pass places which are subject to observation and which are particularly dangerous during daylight, parts of the unit will be deployed to provide protection until the unit has passed. Then they will rejoin the units as soon as possible. At night, silence in all movements is an important factor. The direction of the wind may be decisive in selecting a route of approach. In moonlight the march should follow a shadowed route as much as possible in order to provide concealment from the enemy.

Within range of the enemy, it is necessary to decide whether skis should be kept on or stacked, how far hand sleds may go, and whether snowshoes should be put on. In order to obtain cover and concealment, it is often necessary to use detours or terrain unfavorable for skiing. The troops then march on foot or on snowshoes. An attempt must be made at all times to gain, under cover, heights from which it will be possible to make a rapid descent through terrain which is under fire or observation.

c. Tactics

Combat and tactical measures depend on the mission and the enemy situation. Ski patrols on a reconnaissance mission fight only if it is necessary for the accomplishment of the mission, or if the situation is momentarily favorable.

The missions of ski assault units and raiding parties generally require bold and sudden execution. The aim must be to give the enemy no rest at any time and to weaken and paralyze his fighting power without enabling him to utilize his numerical superiority. Skillful and versatile leadership may annihilate a much stronger enemy or at least inflict heavy losses on him. In woods and at night small detachments may shake the morale of the enemy tremendously through mobile and surprise attacks. Careful preparation and lightning action are the basis for success of all missions of this kind.

The strength and location of the enemy as well as the terrain he occupies must be carefully reconnoitered before entering battle. Strict care must be taken, however, to see that the contemplated action is not guessed by the enemy. An engagement will always be opened by surprise fire. The more suddenly it hits the enemy and the less he is able to take quick defensive measures, the more effective it will be. Opening fire too early often means saving the enemy from complete annihilation.

To deceive the enemy with regard to the strength of the attacking unit, it may be practical to stage the attack on a broad front or with several detachments firing simultaneously from several directions. If possible, the combat position will be established in terrain which is unfavorable for hostile counterattack but which permits the ski unit to shift or withdraw under cover.

Ski patrols, assault units, or raiding parties are not suited for a prolonged engagement, because of their usually limited ammunition supply. They detach themselves from the enemy after forcing a decision, or complete his destruction in close combat.

Night is generally best for carrying out harassing missions. It facilitates disengaging from the enemy after completion of a mission in order to increase his confusion by attacking him again elsewhere. The attack should be made from a direction that will facilitate the cutting of the enemy's communications with his rear. If sufficient forces are available, total encirclement of the enemy is most likely to succeed. If a mission has failed or only partially succeeded, the leader decides whether or not the mission will be continued, repeated at another point, or abandoned.

d. Disengaging Actions

Disengaging from the enemy is an essential part of operations and must be provided for in the operational plan of the leader of a ski patrol, assault unit, or raiding party. At times the return may prove more difficult than the approach.

The method of evacuation depends on the situation and terrain. It is carried out by a simultaneous withdrawal of all elements, or, in order to provide covering fire, a gradual withdrawal. In a gradual withdrawal the leader designates the men and weapons which remain in contact with the enemy, usually under his direction. As long as the raiding party is under fire, it will retreat, if possible, on previously prepared tracks made from one assembly point to another, as designated by the leader. Ski tracks often remain visible for a long time and betray the route. Therefore, the enemy must be deceived as to the return route by dummy tracks, loops, and false route signs.

In newly fallen snow the tracks may be blurred by spruce branches dragged by the last skier. If the enemy pursues, as many delays as possible must be arranged for him. These include sudden fire from ambush, trail-breaking through difficult terrain, preparation of road blocks and obstacles, and mining of trails.

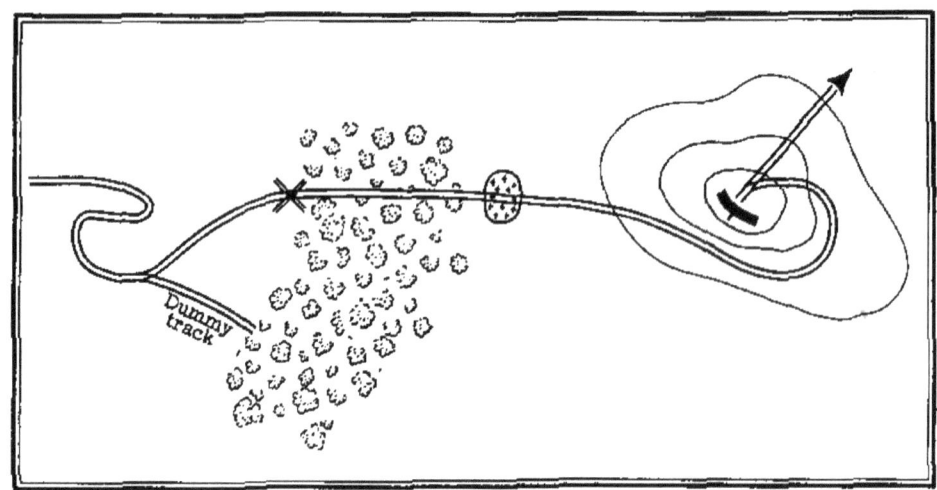

Figure 28.—Ambush position on a ridge.

If possible, ambush positions will be established on ridges from which it is possible to direct effective enfilading fire at the enemy during his slow ascent, while the troops not yet in position dodge quickly to the rear (fig. 28).

Section VI. SKI COMPANY AND SKI BATTALION

23. ORGANIZATION AND EMPLOYMENT

a. General

Ski companies and ski battalions are units organized by the field forces at the beginning of winter in accordance with directives issued by higher headquarters. They are, as organizations which remain mobile in snow, particularly suitable for offensive missions in winter warfare. Some ski battalions are formed by the Army High Command and maintained as GHQ troops. They are designated as *Jäger* battalions[1] and their companies as light and heavy weapons *Jäger* companies. (For details on organization, see appendix A, p. 74.)

Ski troops are the most mobile arm of the infantry in snow-covered terrain, and they are best utilized in combat away from roads. Because of their special training and equipment, ski troops can execute combat missions lasting several days without support from other forces and independent of supply from higher echelons.

The possibilities for employment of ski troops depend to a high degree on their state of training. The ski unit must be specially trained before it may be committed. The more advanced the training, the harder may be the tasks assigned to the unit.

b. Training Principles

The aim of training must be to achieve skiing proficiency as well as a high standard of military training in general. Short ski courses should supplement the training of the less proficient skiers. Development of endurance and of a good, effortless cross-country

---

[1] Light infantry battalions. See the reference to the *Jäger* battalion in the preface, p. IV.)—EDITOR.

style will be specially stressed. Training in pulling hand sleds and preparing tracks will be combined with skiing instruction.

The success of a ski unit depends primarily on its mobility and speed. The training of the soldier and of all subordinate leaders must be guided by this principle. The condition of ski and sled equipment is also decisively important. Care of this equipment is as important as the care of weapons.

The objective of training in weapons and tactics must be defined clearly and kept within proper limits in order to cover all the manifold aspects of winter warfare within the short time available. Officers, noncommissioned officers, and other enlisted men possessing special proficiency or experience in winter operations will be put on detached service as soon as possible and used as instructors and coaches for the ski unit, regardless of rank.

In training the individual rifleman, the most important thing is marksmanship. The various firing positions will be practiced with and without skis. Training as sharpshooters with rifles equipped with telescopic sights, and with semiautomatic rifles, will be particularly stressed. Every man must be trained in the use of the light machine gun and the submachine gun. A knowledge of the most common infantry weapons of the enemy is desirable.

Training in the combat firing of light and heavy infantry weapons will be practiced under difficult conditions (after long marches, at night, in difficult terrain). Crews of heavy weapons in particular, by frequent firing exercises in snow-covered terrain, must be accustomed to firing in the conditions peculiar to winter. Operational training must stress combat under special conditions. The following training subjects will be practiced in detail:

(1) Training of ski patrols, ski assault units, and raiding parties.
(2) Marching as advance, rear, and flank guard of road-bound forces.
(3) Quick occupation of key points (missions of spearhead units).
(4) Envelopment and flanking pursuit of the road-bound enemy.
(5) Screening of the movements and the assembly of friendly forces.
(6) Mobile defense on a broad front.
(7) Annihilation of guerrillas, paratroopers, and airborne troops in trackless terrain.

Strenuous marches, including night bivouacs lasting several days, will be incorporated in the training schedule at an early date.

During these exercises, peacetime comforts will not be permitted. Night marching and fighting, and combat in woods and villages must be specially practiced.

Officers and noncommissioned officers will be trained to lead their troops in all kinds of weather, with emphasis on the special requirements of ski troops. Training in making rapid decisions, such as are necessary while commanding independent units (reinforced company, raiding party, scouting patrol) are to be stressed. Map exercises and terrain discussions will be included frequently for the purpose of preparing and intensifying the practical combat training of platoons, companies, and battalions. All officers and noncommissioned officers must be proficient in every weapon of the ski company.

The training of the individual soldier covers—

(1) First aid for wounds and frostbites.
(2) Preparation of meals in the field.
(3) Cutting and improving roads and paths in winter, and constructing improvised shelters and simple obstacles.
(4) Russian winter tactics and climatic conditions of the Eastern Front.

Drivers and sled crews, besides receiving instruction in the driving of horse-drawn sleds and the care of horses, must also be trained as individual riflemen and sentries, and in the use of hand grenades. Physical training and instruction in recreational skiing are conducted primarily for physical conditioning and for increasing proficiency in skiing.

c. Principles of Command

Ski-troop officers of all ranks must possess great agility, hardiness, willingness to accept responsibility, and initiative. They must share physical hardships and privations with their troops. They must be familiar with the climatic conditions of the theater of operations and have adequate knowledge of the special employment and capacities of ski troops.

In every situation advantage will be taken of favorable climatic conditions. It is desirable to attack the enemy whenever he is most fatigued, but to lead our own troops into battle when they are as well rested as possible.

Surprise and deception of the enemy are decisively important for ski troops. These factors are made possible through utilization of the long nights and poor visibility, and, above all, through the superior mobility of ski troops in almost any type of winter terrain.

Since it is difficult for ski troops to take artillery along, they must frequently accomplish their missions without artillery support. To gain fire superiority, therefore, it is necessary to stress concentration of the fire of light and heavy infantry weapons as well as the combined flat and high-trajectory fire on the point where the main effort is made. The necessary limitation on the number of weapons will be made up by increasing the allotment of ammunition.

24. OPERATIONS

a. Reconnaissance and Security

The ski unit, whose missions usually lead into unknown terrain and unreconnoitered situations, is in great danger of being surprised by the enemy. Unceasing reconnaissance and security efforts and an ever alert eye are therefore prime requisites for all operations. Even great fatigue of the troops must not be permitted as an excuse for neglect of necessary measures for reconnaissance and security.

Preparatory to the attack, reconnaissance will be made on a broad front in such a manner that the enemy cannot draw any conclusions as to the direction of the assault. Full advantage will be taken of every opportunity to deceive the enemy by pseudo-reconnaissance and by leading enemy observation and security into a wrong direction. Twilight and bright nights must be utilized for reconnaissance in the same manner as daylight.

Well-camouflaged observers must supplement reconnaissance efforts within the range of their vision. In snow-covered terrain, the enemy cannot forever evade conscientious and thorough observation. Observation also contributes to the security of the unit in bivouac, on the march, and in combat.

Intelligence on winter road nets behind the enemy front is especially important, not only in determining the direction of our own assault but also that of the enemy. Reconnaissance of enemy terrain will therefore stress roads and trails available to the enemy. They must be marked on maps and road sketches right on the spot.

Safe transmission of orders and messages, and contact between patrols by means of identification and communication signals, must be regulated by order. (See appendix E, par. **36**, p. 100.)

b. Attack

In snow-covered terrain, a road-bound enemy will be hard hit by an attack against his flank and rear, and, above all, against his rear communications. Therefore, the enveloping attack, utilizing the mobility afforded by skis, is the most effective type of action for ski troops. Against an enemy who is already shaken or who is not prepared for defense, a bold frontal attack may also be successful.

The purpose of the enveloping attack is the encirclement of the enemy. Therefore, the forces committed frontally will generally be weak ones, while the enveloping forces will be strong. The attack is carried out according to the plan ordered by the battalion or company commander, the plan being based on the results of reconnaissance and observation. It will be communicated promptly to leaders of all units concerned and, if possible, will be supplemented by an overlay. Personal conferences of the unit leaders contribute to a detailed understanding of the cooperative tasks of the various units and weapons.

Moving into the assembly area may be expedited by cutting trails in advance. The units assigned to break trails also take over local security in the assembly area. For this purpose, they will be equipped with light machine guns. If the approach to the assembly area under cover is impossible, it may be advisable, in order to deceive the enemy or to cause him to split up his fire power, to trickle into the assembly area singly or in small groups at irregular intervals, each man breaking his own trail. This method, however, requires considerably more time and will be employed only if the weather permits a long stay in the area.

Heavy infantry weapons and artillery pieces will be placed sufficiently forward at the beginning of the operation in order to enable them to support the attacking troops from their initial positions as long as possible. Because of the difficulty of moving them during combat, they will be placed in position as soon as practicable in accordance with the operational order. Rapid changes of position are facilitated by preparing tracks in advance to the new positions.

The urge to speed the attack must not result in insufficient preparation. In determining time factors, it must be remembered that the emplacement of heavy weapons and the preparation for firing all weapons usually takes twice as long in deep snow and severe cold as under ordinary conditions. All preparations (reconnaissance of the assembly area and observation posts, locations of firing positions, breaking of trails, etc.) must therefore be started early.

It may be advisable to echelon in depth in the assembly area the forces which are to carry out an envelopment, or to give them an advantage in time at the beginning of the attack. To retain mobility, they must usually forego support by heavy weapons, but they must be amply equipped with automatic weapons. It is advisable to attach heavy weapons observers and, if the occasion arises, artillery observers.

Infantry always moves last into the assembly area. The time interval between the completion of the assembly and the beginning of the attack must be kept to a minimum, because lying around in cold and snow is extraordinarily weakening.

The time of attack will not always be the same, but will be changed frequently to deceive the enemy. Attacks at night or during periods of poor visibility are best to gain surprise and to minimize losses. They require, however, particularly careful preparation, including, if possible, daylight reconnaissance of the terrain and of enemy positions. Objectives of night attacks should not necessitate long approaches.

Enveloping attacks will be executed with simultaneous reconnaissance in front and at the flank in order to enable the enveloping force to by-pass the hostile flanks under maximum cover and to encircle the enemy completely. Bold and determined leadership and a high degree of protection for the flanks of the enveloping forces are the basis of success. The encirclement is further tightened by means of minor attacks from other directions; meanwhile, covering forces must be employed for defense against hostile attempts to relieve the pressure. A few squads armed with machine guns will usually suffice for this purpose. As the encirclement becomes tighter, it may be advisable to force the enemy to stage costly frontal counterattacks in deep snow, or to whittle him down and destroy him by further systematic attacks.

An attack through defenses in depth should be subdivided into several successive stages, each with a short-range objective. The objectives should be selected with the aim of using each, as it is occupied, as the assembly area for the continuation of the attack against the next objective.

c. Pursuit

The superiority of a well-trained, swift-moving ski unit is most effective in pursuit, and superior leadership can gain decisive successes by pursuit.

A flanking pursuit over unguarded, pathless terrain, combined with a frontal pursuit on roads, is the most effective combat technique. To increase mobility, some equipment, heavy weapons, and sleds must frequently be left behind. An effort must always be made during the pursuit to cut off the enemy from his route of retreat, enveloping him on both flanks and forcing him into a small area. As soon as the encircling ski troops are relieved by other troops, the ski units resume the pursuit on both sides of the route of retreat.

The pursuit will be continued day and night, as long as possible. Numerous patrols will be continuously dispatched in order to keep contact with the enemy, and, by means of ambushes and by blocking his routes of retreat, to inflict losses upon him constantly.

d. Defense

The basis of the power of the ski unit in defense is its operational mobility. It is the responsibility of all commanders to retain mobility even during long periods of defensive action. When defending on a broad front, strong reserves of ski assault troops, held ready for action, will take the place of a uniform and complete distribution of troops along the main line of resistance.

The backbone of the defense will consist of strongpoints placed far to the front and suitable for all-around defense. Heavy weapons, with ample ammunition, should be emplaced in the strongpoints. No-man's-land is reconnoitered by numerous ski patrols, operating day and night at various hours, and the positions must be safeguarded by protective trails. (See par. **8d,** p. 30.)

Dummy installations, which are quickly and easily constructed in snow-covered terrain, will be employed in large numbers. Camouflage must be used to protect all changes in terrain, such as ski tracks and construction of shelters.

Reconnaissance must be intensified when the front is broad and the strongpoints are few. Early recognition of enemy attacks, especially tank attacks, may be decisively important for successful defense. Tracks must be prepared in advance to make possible a quick change of the positions of heavy weapons.

Frequent actions of ski assault units and raiding parties should be made against the front and the rear of the enemy to disturb him, to weaken his power of resistance, and to force him to spread his forces thinly. At times it may be possible to interfere with, delay or destroy completely enemy concentrations by bold assaults.

To engage an enemy approaching or breaking into the main combat zone, reserve assault troops on skis will be held ready by battalion and company commanders for quick commitment along prepared tracks at the threatened position. Until they are committed, they should stay, if possible, under cover in shelters or dugouts in order that they may enter combat warm and rested.

Counterattacks, when possible, will be directed against the flank of the attacking enemy, who must be annihilated with concentrated fire at close and point-blank range and in hand-to-hand combat.

Especially effective is a pincer-type counterattack, executed by several reserve assault columns for the purpose of encircling an enemy who has broken into the main battle position.

In preparing a counterattack, one must take into consideration the various possibilities for enemy attacks. The counterattack must be systematically practiced while in position.

e. Withdrawal from Action

Withdrawal from action is greatly facilitated by the mobility of ski troops and can often be carried out in daylight without special danger. This is almost always possible if the position can be evacuated by means of a downhill run while the enemy is forced to reach the positions by a long climb. Tracks for the departure must be prepared early.

The order of withdrawal from positions depends on the mobility of the respective weapons. As a rule, the heavy weapons, loaded on sleds, are the first to be withdrawn and, if the situation permits, will be used from rearward positions to cover the retirement of troops remaining in position longest. Rallying positions will be prepared by advance detachments.

Further retreat is carried out in accordance with directives contained in paragraph **22d**, page 57. Especially effective combat patrols will be detailed for flank security.

f. Support and Cooperation

Only very limited employment of horse-drawn and motorized artillery by ski units can be made off the roads. To carry out a mission in which artillery support is advisable, single pieces will be mounted on runners and sleds to make them mobile enough to accompany ski troops, even over difficult terrain. Light guns, dismantled and loaded on sleds, can follow the ski unit in any terrain.

If light gun units are not available, the ski unit, as a rule, will have to do without artillery support if the mobility of the unit is reduced by taking heavy guns along, and if artillery support from advanced initial firing positions is impossible.

Because of the greater difficulties in observation and location of targets in snow-covered terrain, it is necessary to detail additional advanced observers. The principles for commitment and use of single artillery pieces are generally the same as those for infantry howitzers. (See par. **10c**, p. 34.) In areas threatened by air attack, attachment of antiaircraft units to larger ski organizations will prove necessary. Their mobility, even off roads and prepared trails, must be assured by equipping them with sleds or runners.

Assault-gun units are excellent for support of ski units if terrain and snow conditions are favorable. They can move through snow 12 inches deep without material loss of speed. If, however, the snow is deeper than the ground clearance of the vehicles (16 inches and up), their speed begins to decrease rapidly. Snow more than 29 inches deep cannot, as a rule, be negotiated by assault guns. When the snow is too deep, it may be necessary to use shovels in clearing approaches for such guns when they are employed in attacks with limited objectives.

To save effort, assault guns may be used in suitable terrain to tow accompanying ski infantry. (See appendix B, par. **29**, p. 83.) In an attack, the troops thus towed also furnish added local protection for the pieces.

The employment of assault-gun units in winter is extremely dependent on terrain and snow conditions; therefore, they require close cooperation and extensive support from the ski unit. In particular, engineers must be assigned for clearing roads for the pieces, for removing mines, for early reconnaissance of the carrying capacity of bridges or frozen bodies of water and of the depth of snow. Because of the difficulty of target recognition in snowy terrain, range-finding by accompanying infantry assumes increased importance.

Attached tanks and assault guns will, as a matter of principle, be employed in platoon or company strength, never singly.

The flexible employment of the ski unit requires exact compliance with regulations concerning cooperation with the Air Force. All members of the ski unit must be familiar with the meaning of, and rules for, the use of identification signals and codes between ground forces and air units.

If a ski unit has penetrated deep into the enemy lines, it may be advantageous to indicate not only front lines but also flank and rear boundaries of the marching or fighting unit with panels, smoke signals, or swastika flags. Support by aircraft in lieu of artillery, which is rarely available, assumes greater importance for ski units. Targets must be clearly designated by tracers and panels.

Long-range missions may temporarily necessitate supply of the ski unit by airplanes. Panels for the place where supplies are to be dropped will, wherever possible, be placed in open terrain far enough away from the front line to conceal them from enemy ground observation, but plainly visible from the air. They must be removed promptly if enemy aircraft approaches.

g. Cooperation with Infantry on Foot

The ski unit can give considerable support to infantry on foot because, being independent of roads, it may be committed quickly. It is the responsibility of the combined command to coordinate the commitment of the rapidly moving ski unit with the operations of the unit marching on foot. The principles of combat and command of the ski unit are not changed when they are employed in combination with units marching on foot.

Employment of the ski unit in this connection covers mainly the following points:

(1) Reconnaissance and security measures over extensive areas.
(2) Screening of movements and security of friendly forces while they are assembling.
(3) Employment as flank and rear enveloping forces.
(4) Employment in pursuit and rear-guard actions.

In missions within range of friendly artillery, operations of the ski unit can be considerably facilitated by artillery support. In such cases, the commander will request either an artillery liaison detail, made mobile by means of skis and hand sleds, or artillery observers.

25. SPECIAL OPERATIONS

a. Actions behind Enemy Lines

If a ski unit is ordered to perform a mission behind the enemy lines, it must first determine by reconnaissance on a broad front whether there is a gap in the enemy position through which it is possible to pass without detection, or whether it is possible to by-pass an enemy flank without engaging the enemy. As a rule, missions of this type can be carried out only in darkness or foggy weather.

If the enemy shows a solid front, it might become advisable for the ski unit to force its way through the enemy lines by systematic attack. To support this attack, the concentrated fire of artillery and all available heavy weapons not accompanying the ski unit will be utilized against the point selected for penetration, and also will be employed to screen the flanks. Depending on the circumstances, part of the infantry may also accompany the ski unit in the attack to effect the break-through. The infantry returns to its position after the penetration has been completed.

The most favorable time for missions behind enemy lines is during the early evening hours. This affords the ski unit considerable time during which it may penetrate, under cover of darkness, far into the enemy's rear without being detected. Further actions depend on the mission. The principles of operations of raiding parties (par. **22**, p. 54) apply largely to actions behind the enemy lines.

If adequate concealment, such as wooded terrain, is lacking, movements in the enemy's rear will usually be made only in darkness. The unit must be specially secured by a rear point and strong flank guards. During the day, troops will bivouac in remote, concealed positions. Inhabited places will be avoided.

The bivouac area must be equipped for all-around defense, and it must be guarded in all directions. During extended missions, bivouacs suitable as points of departure for several operations can be converted into supply dumps. (See par. **26a** and **b**, p. 72.)

Radio equipment is usually the only means of communication with the main unit. Its use must be precisely prescribed in advance. In order to impede efforts of the enemy to search for and locate our radio equipment by radio-location finders, transmitting schedules and frequencies will be changed daily. Sending in the clear is forbidden.

For the return march, it is advisable to select a different route, which, if possible, will have been chosen and reconnoitered during the approach. If circumstances permit, friendly troops, if they were not advised before the operation, must be informed in advance of the manner and time of return. During the return march, as during the approach march, it may be necessary to penetrate the enemy lines by attack from the rear. The unit then could not usually rely on effective support from the artillery and heavy weapons which have remained in position.

b. Combat against Guerrillas and Special Units

Combat against enemy bands, paratroops, and airborne troops in winter is one of the most essential tasks of the ski unit. The principles of combat and leadership of the ski unit will be applied in every detail against these enemy units. Because of its great mobility in winter, the ski unit is able to locate with relative speed an enemy who is usually operating in trackless terrain, and to annihilate him by systematically prepared attacks, executed as surprise actions. The objective of the attacks must be, above all, the raiding and destruction of hostile operating bases and shelters. Actions against enemy groups become most effective once they have been cut off from their bases and are exposed to cold and difficulties of supply.

In winter, ski and sled tracks give away the location of the enemy's hiding places even at great distances and disclose information concerning his strength and disposition. Even when organizing reconnaissance forces, it must be borne in mind that all hostile forces operating in the rear of our lines are especially tough and shrewd fighters.

26. SUPPLY

a. Means of Supply

Methods of supplying ski units depend largely on the situation, the terrain, the condition of the winter roads, and snow and weather conditions. They may be different for each undertaking; hence the manner in which the troops will be supplied will be stated precisely in every tactical order.

The motor vehicles of the second echelon of the ration train of the ski battalion can take care of the supply of the fighting unit only so far as the enemy situation and the condition of winter roads permit. As a rule, it will be necessary to establish a distributing point for companies in the forward area for supplies drawn from ration and ammunition depots. This may necessitate the use of horse-drawn sleds.

The company, as a rule, uses the first-echelon ration train, equipped with horse-drawn sleds, for its supply. If, because of the tactical situation or terrain or snow conditions, horse-drawn sleds cannot be used, an adequate number of hand sleds will be substituted. Dog teams (see appendix B, par. **31,** p. 86) may prove particularly useful.

Sled echelons supplying companies must be in a position to defend themselves against hostile attack. They will always be equipped with light machine guns and submachine guns. When necessary, they will be further protected by guard details.

b. Supply Dumps

The establishment of supply dumps between receiving and distributing points depends on the length of the supply lines as well as on the difficulties of terrain and snow conditions. Often supply dumps must be set up even by small units (raiding parties and patrols), which, being absent for several days from their units while on special missions, cannot be supplied through regular supply channels and are unable to take the necessary supply of rations and ammunition along.

Dumps must be prepared along the route of approach at such intervals that the distance between dumps, or between dump and receiving or distributing point, is not more than a day's march. If sufficient means of transportation are available, supply can be accelerated by shuttle traffic between dumps, and between dumps and receiving and distributing points, in which case the distance between the individual dumps should not exceed half a day's march.

In the selection of dump sites, attention must be given to the storage of supplies in places which are well camouflaged and protected as well as possible from frost. Best suited are shacks and small woods which are a short distance off the route of approach. Wind shelters for horses may have to be provided. In terrain threatened by the enemy, conditions may arise when dumps will have to be guarded continually and in adequate strength. If no special snow-shoveling details have been organized, guards will keep open the supply and approach routes in the vicinity of the supply dumps.

Appendix A. ORGANIZATION: SKI COMPANY AND BATTALION

27. ORGANIZATION OF THE SKI COMPANY

a. General

The ski company is the one organization within the infantry regiment which is fully mobile in winter. It is formed by regimental order from the organic components of the war-strength regiment which furnish personnel on a quota basis. If a sufficient number of trained skiers and the necessary special winter equipment are available, a ski company may be formed, in reduced strength if necessary, in each infantry battalion.

Only trained skiers may be assigned to the ski company. Nonskiers impair the mobility and fighting power of the ski unit to a considerable degree and are not suitable, even if they possess the other fighting qualities required. Officers, noncommissioned officers, and enlisted men who are proficient in skiing and who wish to volunteer are given preferential consideration. If a single unit has a particularly large number of skiers, it should furnish the entire cadre of the ski company.

The quotas within a two-battalion regiment and a three-battalion regiment may be fixed as follows:

(1) *Two-battalion regiment.—*

1st battalion	Company headquarters, 1st platoon, heavy mortar section.
2d battalion	2d and 3d platoons, combat train, Ration Train I.
Infantry howitzer company	Baggage train.

(2) *Three-battalion regiment.*—

1st battalion	Company headquarters, 1st platoon, combat train.
2d battalion	2d platoon, 1 heavy mortar squad, baggage train.
3d battalion	3d platoon, 1 heavy mortar squad, Ration Train I.

The antitank company, the regimental signal platoon, the mounted platoon, and the bicycle platoon may also be called upon to furnish detachments. The same method of proportionate quotas is followed when a ski company is formed within a battalion.

As soon as the ski company is formed, its specialized training begins. Units formed from several organizations require a longer time for training. Poorly trained skiers must improve their skiing by means of short courses in technique.

The parent unit is responsible for providing the ski company with as much fire power and mobility as possible. If a ski company is used as an independent unit within the framework of the regiment and not as part of a ski battalion, it is reinforced by attaching heavy weapons. If its own resources are inadequate, additional personnel and equipment will be procured from other units through the proper authorities.

The organization chart shown in figure 29 is based on the light *Jäger*[1] company of the *Jäger* battalion (GHQ) with three rifle platoons and one heavy mortar section. Changes in strength and composition may be made in keeping with the combat strength of the parent units.

b. Peculiarities of Organization

The following peculiarities of organization may be noted:

(1) The strength of the rifle squad is increased by 2 men, making a total of 1 squad leader and 11 men.

(2) The light mortar squads are omitted.

(3) One light machine gun is assigned to the combat train.

(4) Buglers and bicyclists of the company or platoon headquarters are detailed as messengers.

---

[1] See par. **23**, p. 59.—EDITOR.

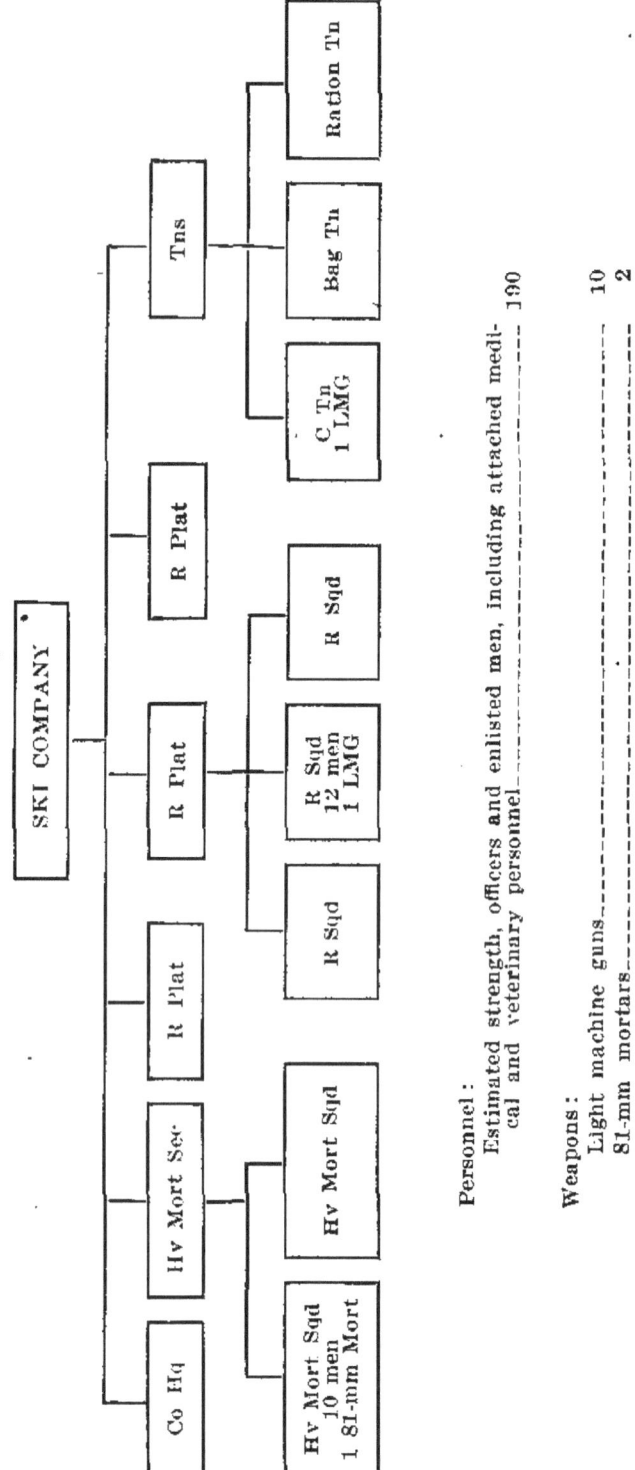

Figure 29.—Organization of the ski company.

ORGANIZATION: SKI COMPANY AND BATTALION

(5) The number of men in the heavy mortar section is increased to 20.[2]

(6) The number of litter bearers and medical personnel is doubled, and a medical officer is attached to the company if the additional personnel are available.

(7) Riflemen and ammunition bearers of the squads are detailed to pull the hand sleds.

c. Arms and Ammunition

At least 2 semiautomatic rifles should be issued to each squad. At least 1 rifle in each squad should be equipped with a telescopic sight. Submachine guns are issued to every commander, assistant commander, and squad leader (including the leaders of the trains). The issue of rifle ammunition is increased to 100 rounds for each man. There is also an increased issue of armor-piercing tracer ammunition, signal ammunition and flares, hand grenades, explosives and fuzes. Ten percent of the heavy mortar grenades are smoke grenades. The squad is equipped with a tripod mount so that the light machine gun may be used as a heavy machine gun. All weapons are camouflaged with white covers or white paint.

d. Clothing and Equipment

(1) *Clothing.*—Winter combat suits are issued if they are available; otherwise the following are issued: mountain trousers or long trousers; ski or laced shoes (large enough for three pairs of socks); short puttees or ski gaiters; camouflage suit or camouflage cloak; three sets of woolen underwear; additional protective clothing (pullovers, sweaters, belly bands, and jock straps); one pair of gloves and one pair of woolen mittens; no overcoats, but three woolen blankets instead (two with the combat train); no steel helmet, but cap with white cover instead; face mask and snow goggles (if available).

(2) *Bivouac equipment.*—Twenty-man tents with small stoves are issued (if available); otherwise pyramidal tents (which can be improvised by sewing shelter halves together) and waterproof

---

[2] A German heavy mortar section normally consists of 18 men: 2 squads of 6 men each and a headquarters of 6 men. However, it is believed that the increase referred to here applies to the gun crews only: 20 gunners instead of 12. Thus the section in a ski unit would total 26 men.—EDITOR.

ground sheets (canvas and captured shelter halves) are issued. Fuel is to be taken along in country without woods. Small field kitchens installed on one-horse sleds (with a capacity of 500 kilograms (1,102 pounds)) are issued (if available); otherwise thermos bottles are issued. Two gasoline (*Benzin* or *Esbit*) stoves are issued to every squad for cooking and heating purposes. Fewer spades and more hand saws and hatchets instead should be taken.

(3) *Medical equipment.*—One tent with a stove is issued for each company for the wounded, as well as one hand sled for each platoon for transportation of the wounded, and an increased amount of bandages, antifrostbite medicines, and stimulants.

(4) *Ski and sled equipment.*—(a) *Ski equipment.*—With the exception of the drivers of horse-drawn sleds, every man of the ski company will be equipped with 1 ski set (1 pair of skis, 1 pair of poles, 1 spare binding). Every 10 men will be issued 1 ski kit containing 1 spare tip, 1 pair of ski climbers, straps and wire for binding, repair tools, various kinds of ski wax, and 1 spare ski set.

If possible, employ skis without steel edges but with adjustable bindings, unless the skis are equipped with the Army flat-terrain ski binding (*Kuncekbindung*). Bamboo ski poles are issued to trained skiers; others are issued hazel poles. When ski climbers are issued, towing crews will be given priority.

(b) *Snowshoes.*—Snowshoes will be issued to drivers of horse-drawn sleds and to men who lead horses; to each squad, also, are issued three pairs (for men towing sleds and for use as bases for the light machine gun).

(c) *Hand sleds.*—The average number of hand sleds issued to the ski company is 9 weapons akjas and 18 boat akjas. At least 1 weapons akja (open hand sled) is issued to each squad, and 1 boat akja (closed hand sled) to each platoon and company headquarters; 8 boat akjas are issued to the heavy mortar section. Additional hand sleds are issued, depending on the number and the towing crews available.

(d) *Horse-drawn sleds.*—In place of horse-drawn wagons, one-horse sleds with a capacity of 250, 300, and 500 kilograms (551, 661, and 1,102 pounds, respectively) are furnished. The 500-kilogram sleds (for trains only) may be hauled by horses in tandem. It is important that all horse-drawn sleds be of standard gauge, with wide, smooth running surfaces.

28. ORGANIZATION OF THE SKI BATTALION

a. General

The ski battalion is the one organization within the division which is fully mobile in winter. It is formed by division order from the organic components of the war-strength division. If a sufficient number of trained skiers and the special winter equipment are available, a ski battalion may be formed, in reduced strength if necessary, in each infantry regiment.

In procuring personnel to form the ski battalion of the division, the officers, noncommissioned officers, and other enlisted men who are trained in skiing, as well as the weapons and trains of the bicycle and reconnaissance battalions, are drawn on first. If these sources are not sufficient, the infantry regiments and the other independent units of the division are called on to assign further personnel, weapons, and equipment on a quota basis.

Each ski company will be formed, when possible, *en bloc* from the units of one regiment. The same procedure is followed in forming the platoons of the headquarters company and the heavy weapons company. In the organization of ski unit, the war strength of the division will be changed as little as possible. As a rule, the ski battalion is placed under the direct control of the division.

The organization shown in figure 30 is based upon the composition of a *Jäger* battalion (GHQ) with three light *Jäger* companies, one heavy *Jäger* company, and one headquarters company. Changes in strength and composition may be made in accordance with the combat strength of the parent division.

b. Peculiarities of Organization

(1) *Battalion headquarters.*—If possible, a battalion veterinary and three assistant medical officers will be assigned (one for each ski company). Increase the number of messengers to eight men. Mounted messengers and motorcycle messengers will operate on skis.

(2) Headquarters company.—

Engineer platoon	3 squads, each consisting of 1 noncommissioned officer and 12 other enlisted men.
Signal platoon	2 telephone teams, each consisting of 1 noncommissioned officer and 4 other enlisted men, with "d"[3] equipment; and 8 radio teams each consisting of 1 noncommissioned officer and 2 other enlisted men, with "b"[4] equipment.

(3) Heavy weapons company.—

Heavy machine-gun platoon.	Composed of 3 sections (each machine-gun crew consisting of 1 noncommissioned officer and 6 other enlisted men), 1 machine gun mounted on weapons akja.
Light infantry howitzer.	Piece on runners or special sled.
Heavy antitank-rifle platoon.	Weapons (disassembled) loaded on 4 boat akjas or special sleds.
20-mm antiaircraft platoon.	Weapon on special sled (110-pound capacity); tandem hauling is necessary.

---

[3] Portable telephone transmitter and receiver.—EDITOR.

[4] Portable radio transmitter and receiver.—EDITOR.

ORGANIZATION: SKI COMPANY AND BATTALION

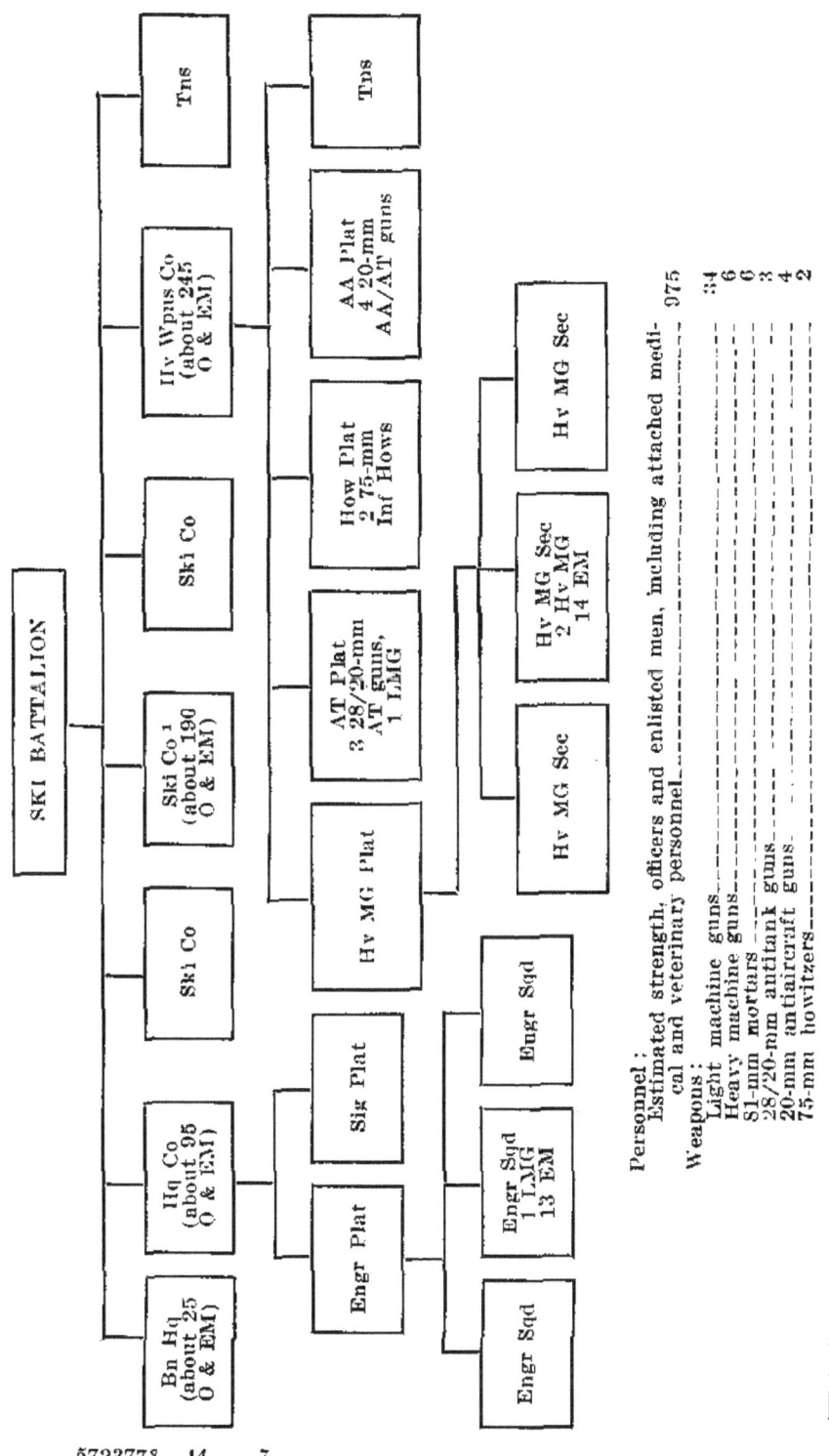

Figure 30.—Organization of the ski battalion.

Appendix B. TOWING, SNOWSHOEING, AND DOG TEAMS

29. TOWING SKIERS

a. General

Under favorable snow conditions on level ground, there are no special difficulties in towing skiers at moderate speeds behind horses (*Skijöring*). Skiing in tow may be learned easily even by inexperienced skiers. Towing in deep snow, on ice, or on narrow, rough paths requires more practice. Towing by motor vehicles or sleds is done in the same way as skijoring, but favorable snow conditions are necessary, and, because of the increased speed which is possible, longer ski training is required.

The possibilities for towing skiers into combat depend upon the tactical objective, the number of available horses or motor vehicles, and weather and road conditions. Towing is especially suitable for giving mobility to scouting and reconnaissance squads, billeting parties. leaders of units and messengers, and small ski units behind the front line. When employed in cooperation with tanks, skiers can be towed directly into combat by the tanks.

Each horse can normally tow two skiers without losing much endurance. If snow and terrain conditions are favorable, the number of skiers may be increased to four. The towing capacity of horses is only slightly decreased by empty or lightly loaded sleds. Motor vehicles usually can tow a greater number of skiers. Tanks, assault guns. half tracks, and motorcycles equipped with chains are especially suitable.

b. Methods of Towing

The skiers form a double row on either side of the road behind the horse, at intervals of 20 to 25 feet. The horseman thereupon rides between the two rows of skiers, loosens the towropes which are fastened to the trace or saddle, and throws them to the skiers. The skiers put the poles together by slipping one through the ring of the other, hold them with the points outward in their outside hand, grasp the rope, and fasten it around the poles with a half hitch (fig. 31). While in motion, the poles are held with slightly bent arms, horizontally in front of the body, the towrope passing around the outside of the body. A skier, when being towed alone, fastens both ropes to the poles. The lengths of both ropes must be the same in order to keep them taut.

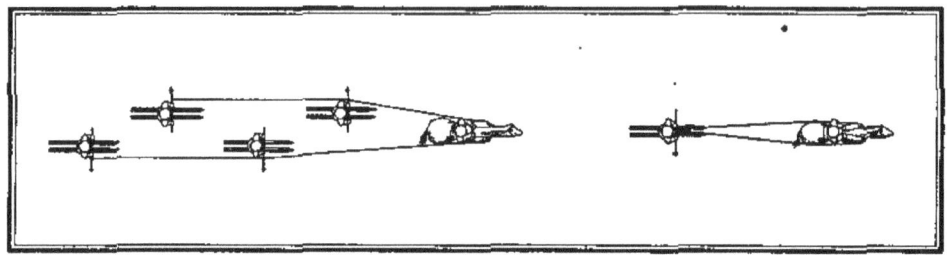

Figure 31.—Skiers being towed by horses.

When the towing is done by motor vehicles and sleds, the skiers form behind the column of vehicles (fig. 32) and manage the ropes in the same manner as skiers towed by horses.

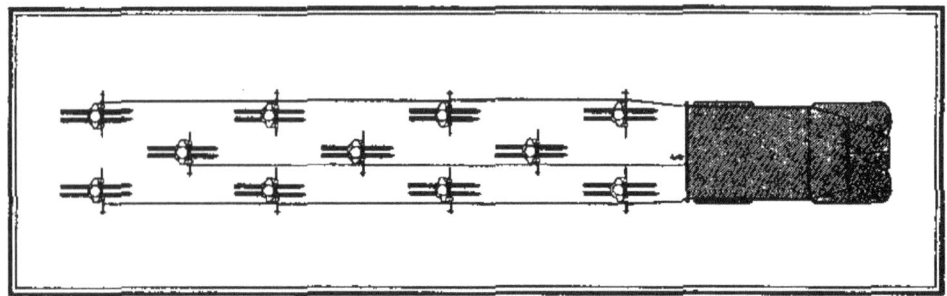

Figure 32.—Skiers being towed by a motor vehicle.

At the end of each column of skiers there must be a collecting detail, which, depending on the composition of the main column, consists of several mounted men, a sled, or a motor vehicle. Its function is to pick up stragglers and to take them back to the column.

TOWING, SNOWSHOEING, AND DOG TEAMS 85

The mounted men start the march at a walk. The normal speed prescribed for the different gaits must be somewhat reduced. Transition from one gait to the other must be gradual. At sharp bends in the road, speed is reduced. When descending on difficult slopes, horses must walk. When riding long distances, a short stop must be made from time to time to adjust the ropes and the grip on the ski poles. Stragglers can rejoin the column during these stops.

Drivers of motor vehicles and sleds must make it a point to start slowly and to increase the speed gradually. Road and snow conditions as well as grades determine the speed. An assistant driver must be assigned to each vehicle to maintain contact between the driver and the skiers. Sudden stops must be avoided, because they can cause the skiers to fall or to crash into the vehicle.

While being towed, the skier holds his body erect, leaning slightly backward, the skis somewhat apart. While in motion, the towing rope is kept taut. Sudden jerks of the rope are offset by flexing the arms.

When climbing, the skier propels himself in order to avoid putting any strain on the horse. When descending, he brakes the speed by stemming. If a skier falls, he immediately lets go of the rope and throws himself to the side, out of the way of the following skiers. He joins the collecting detail or tries to rejoin his unit at the next stop by increasing his speed.

30. SNOWSHOEING

Walking on snowshoes can be learned in a very short time. For nonskiers it is the best means of movement in deep snow. Snowshoes can be used to pack down the snow in making a path or a sled track and they are helpful when pulling sleds up steep slopes. Drivers of horse-drawn sleds should always be equipped with snowshoes.

In combat during especially inclement weather or on unfavorable terrain, snowshoes may also be used temporarily instead of skis. When the snowshoes are being strapped on, they are placed flat on the ground. Remove snow and ice from the buckles and the fastening strap. Place the foot in the middle of the snowshoe and fasten the strap so that the snowshoe is held rigidly on the foot (fig. 33).

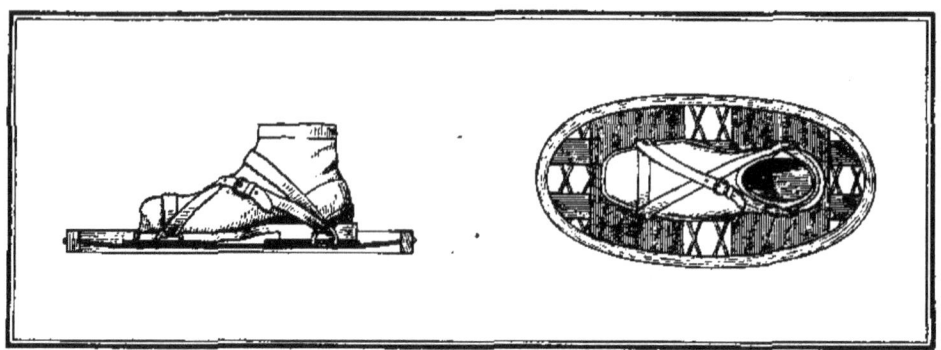

Figure 33.—Method of strapping the snowshoe.

In flat terrain, walk with the toes turned inward, placing the snowshoes flat on the ground. In climbing, kick the toes of the snowshoes in to avoid sliding back. In descending, kick in the heels. When traversing a slope, lift the feet high, edge the snowshoes into the snow, and kick them in firmly.

Breaking trail in deep, loose snow is exhausting work. Therefore, the front men must be relieved frequently. They step to the side and fall in at the end of the column. The use of the ski poles considerably facilitates breaking trail.

31. DOG TEAMS

Dog teams may be used to economize on towing crews in transporting weapons, ammunition, rations, and casualties in any kind of weather and in all reasonably level terrain.

Only trained, reliable, and obedient dogs may be used near the enemy. The sled dogs must be hardened to winter weather and trained in teamwork. Those most suitable are Eskimo, Newfoundland, Siberian, and Lapland dogs. The same dogs will always be used, if possible, in the same sled team. Frequent changing of the drivers detailed to feed and care for the dogs must be avoided.

The dogs must be accustomed to travel up to 12 miles without stopping to feed. If the distances are longer and the pulling difficult, the dogs must be fed in a place which is protected from the wind. An ample food supply must be taken along. A stop for feeding and rest must last at least half an hour.

Leather or web straps leading around the front legs, chest, and back are most suitable as harness. The towline is fastened on the back or on both sides of the dog (fig. 34).

Harness sores must be prevented by good care of the harness (grease it lightly). When long marches are made over ice or frozen snow, cloth rags or pieces of fur must be wrapped around the paws.

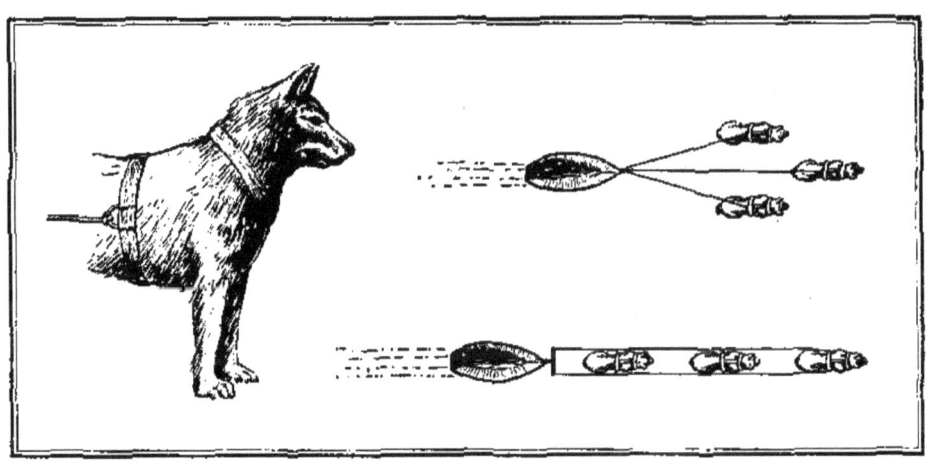

Figure 34.—Methods of harnessing dog teams.

The number of dogs required for a sled depends on the weight of the load. In general, a dog is able to pull the equivalent of its own weight. When a dog team is employed in open terrain, the driver must break trail for the dogs (see fig. 35).

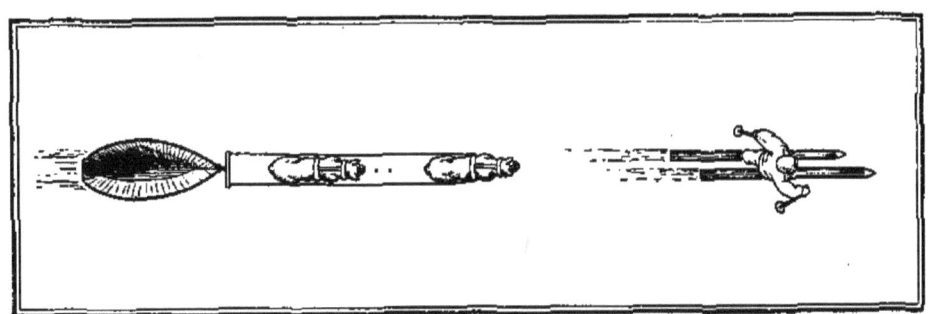

Figure 35.—Driver breaking trail for dogs.

If several dog sleds are employed as a group, one man must be detailed as group leader and one man accompanies each sled. In difficult terrain and when sufficient dogs are not available, the sleds are pulled by men and dogs together (see fig. 36).

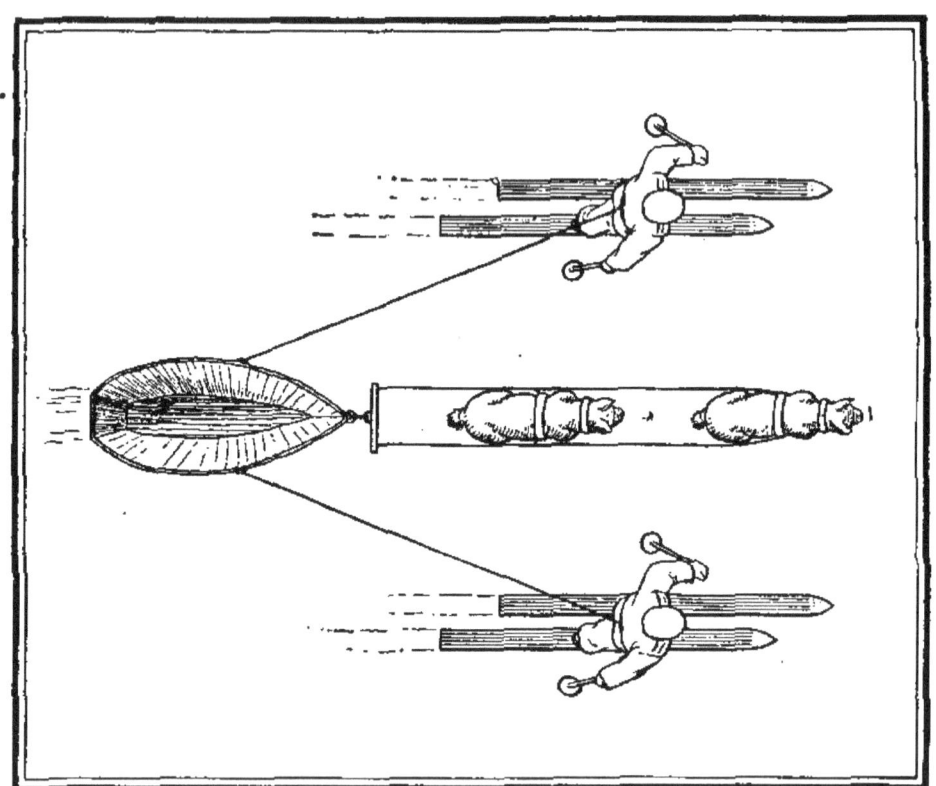

Figure 36.—Men and dogs hauling a sled.

The hauling capacity of the dogs is maintained and improved by frequent employment. If there are no loads to be transported, practice trips must be made, regularly.

Appendix C. MAINTENANCE OF SKIS AND SLEDS

32. CARE OF SKI AND SLED EQUIPMENT

a. General

A ski unit's speed and readiness for action depend essentially on the effectiveness of its ski and sled equipment. The constant and thorough care of this equipment is therefore the duty of all members of ski units; it is equal in importance to the care of weapons and must be given adequate attention in the training and duty schedule. By means of frequent inspections, officers and noncommissioned officers must maintain a continual check on its condition and care. It is especially important, therefore, that all of the ski and sled equipment be checked and repaired with special thoroughness before each action, as even the smallest damage to the equipment can decrease the unit's striking power.

b. Treatment of Ski Surfaces

In order to preserve skis and prolong their life, the running surfaces must be lacquered or treated with a preparation like linseed oil (*Leinöl*), crude pine tar, or wax (*Nassschneewachs*, or *Klister*) with strong tar content. It is best to burn the protective coating into the wood with a torch or with the heat of a wood fire. The running surface of the ski is held over the wood fire. The tar is then carefully rubbed into the wood by hand until the wood is saturated. In this way, the wood pores are closed to dampness, the wax adheres more effectively, and the life of the running surface is prolonged.

c. Waxing

In general, the use of a universal climbing and downhill wax is most practical. The kind and amount of wax used depends on the condition of the snow. It must be evenly distributed by hand and must be rubbed into the wood. It is inadvisable to use a flat iron, because it destroys the properties in the wax which facilitate climbing.

Dry-snow waxes are used for new snow or powdery snow. Thinner layers of wax are applied as the weather gets colder. Damp-snow waxes are used for wet, new snow, sticky snow, and snow around freezing temperature. Wet-snow waxes (*Klister*) are used on melting snow, rained-on snow, hard-packed snow, iced snow, corn snow, and crusted snow. The wetter the snow, the softer should be the wax.

Klister, if applied thinly, can be used even in severe cold as a base for dry-snow wax. If well-covered and properly mixed, it can be used as a base wax around freezing temperature. Remainders of old wax are washed off with gasoline or burned in with a blowtorch or heat from wood embers.

At temperatures below zero the wax must be removed from the running surface. In warmer weather ice and snow which sticks to the running surfaces must be removed with a spatula or a knife, but only in the direction from the heel to the tip. The running surfaces must then be covered with wax.

d. Storing

After the skis have been used, they must be cleaned and examined for damage. They must always be stored with the tips on the ground. If the skis stand on their heels in the snow for long periods, they will absorb moisture in the running surface. If possible, the skis should be strapped together after use, as shown in figure 37. The thickness of the wooden bracing block depends

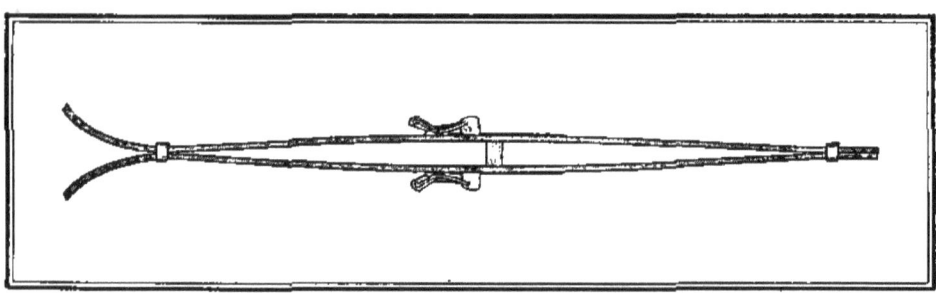

Figure 37.—Method of strapping skis for storage.

on the camber required by the individual skier (the lighter the skier, the less the camber, and vice versa).

The skis are strapped together and either stored flat or placed vertically with the tips on the ground. Damp skis must not be strapped together for 1 to 2 hours after using. Avoid leaving the skis with the running surfaces on the snow for any length of time, or they will get iced. A moderately warm, dry room should be selected for storage. To prevent warping, never dry skis near a stove or an open fire; this would cause them to warp.

e. Repairing

If the skis are inspected and minor repairs are made frequently, serious defects will not develop. Tools, nails, screws, sheet metal (from tin cans), spare tips, and leather straps for webbing must always be carried.

Broken tips are replaced by the spare metal tips. They are patched with sheet metal sleeves made from tin cans. The same general method is used to repair breaks in the running surface. (See fig. 38.)

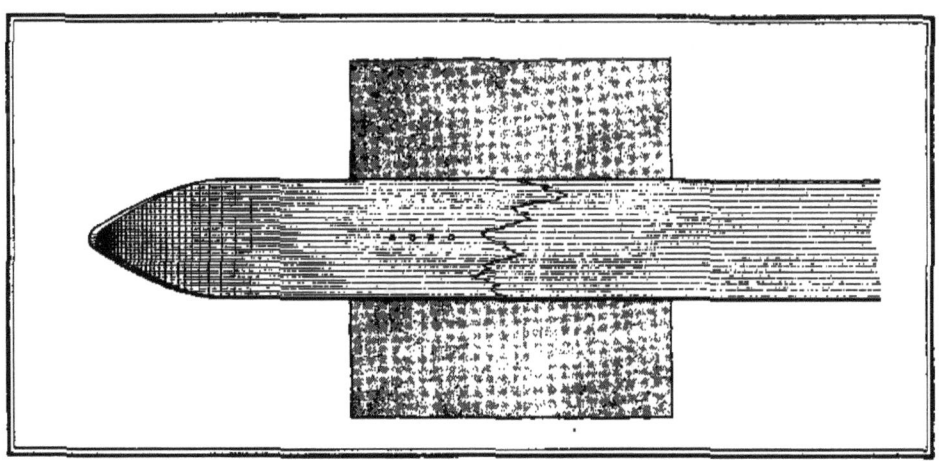

Figure 38.—Method of mending a broken ski tip.

f. Binding

A proper fit of the binding is essential for good skiing performance. The toe irons must be fitted to the edges of the sole on either side of the toes. (Cut round edges straight, if possible;

otherwise fit toe irons to the form of the sole.) The tip of the shoe should not extend more than 1 inch ahead of the front edge of the toe iron. The leather parts of the binding must be kept slightly greased. Too much grease tends to make the leather spongy. Leather should be treated on days when the temperature is above 23 degrees F. Skis should also be treated if they have stood 1 to 2 days in rooms with temperatures above 32 degrees F.

The position of leather strips and cables which run over sharp edges must be changed as often as possible to prevent them from wearing through. The screws of the toe irons must be tested daily and greased. A few threads of wool or wood shavings will keep loose screws tight.

g. Ski Poles

Ski poles, especially cane poles, must be protected against sudden changes in temperature. In storing them, apply the methods prescribed for skis. They must never be dried or stored near stoves or open fires, as this causes splits. The leather parts, like those of the bindings, should be greased only slightly. When the poles begin to split, they can be made almost as strong as before if cord or insulation tape is wrapped around them. When poles are broken, splints should be made for them from branches or other poles.

h. Ski Climbers

Ski climbers must be carefully dried in the open air. The most practical way is to hang them up. They must never be dried near a stove. Small tears at the edges of the ski climbers must be cut away to prevent further tearing.

i. Care of the Sled

The wooden parts of sleds, especially the runners, must be treated with an oil suitable for the purpose (wood-saturation oil). Runners made of metal must be greased frequently with rust-preventing grease. Sleds should not be overloaded or piled too high.

On long marches, the sleds must be checked from time to time and damages must be repaired, loose screws tightened, etc. This should always be done after strenuous use. These precautions will prevent damage which might render the sled at least temporarily useless. The sled must be cleaned of snow and ice after every use and must be placed in a dry spot which is protected from the wind. A foundation of wood and branches under the runners will keep them from freezing.

The leather parts must be greased only slightly. Leather should be treated only on days when the temperature is above 23 degrees F., or after the sleds have been kept from 1 to 2 days in a room with a temperature above 32 degrees F. Leather parts which have frozen hard are best thawed out and dried near a fire (never over an open fire) or in a warm room.

33. TRANSPORTATION OF SKIS

a. Ski Bundle

If terrain conditions and the enemy situation make it necessary to take off the skis and transport them behind the unit, the arrangement of a ski bundle may be ordered to economize on hand sleds and men. In this way it is possible for one man to haul from 8 to 10 pairs of skis over long distances without special help.

In order to make a ski bundle, three to four skis are placed flat on the ground next to each other and tightly fastened together at the bindings by means of a cord. The rest of the skis are placed one on top of the other, the tip of each being pushed under the toe strap of the one below until the binding touches the strap. The skis in the uppermost layer are fastened together with a double towrope, the free end of which is passed in a half hitch around the tips of all the skis stacked on the initial layer. (See fig. 39.)

If the skis have leather bindings, the lower layer can be fastened by means of the bindings themselves. The ski poles are placed in a bundle on top of the uppermost layer of skis and fastened to the bindings by means of a rope.

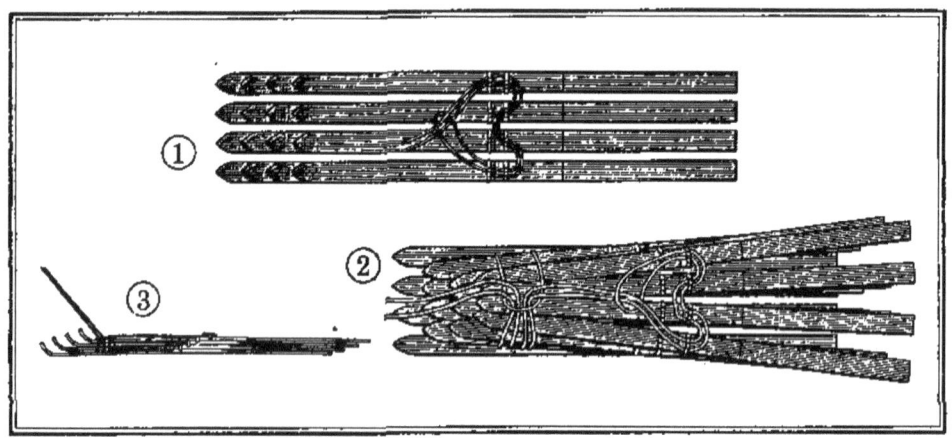

Figure 39.—Method of making a ski bundle.

b. Sliding Ski Bundle

To make a sliding ski bundle for dragging on the snow, one ski of each pair is placed with the heel pointing forward through the toe strap of the other one. Half of the skis which are to be bound are used as the base of the bundle. A rope, 25 to 30 feet long with a loop at the end, is then slipped between the two layers of the paired skis, behind the toe irons of the bindings (fig. 40). The remainder of the skis, in pairs, are placed on this bundle, and the poles are put on top of them. The bundle is then fastened tight by means of one hitch at the bindings and a second hitch 6 or 8 inches from the towing end of the bundle. Two men are required for hauling it.

An effort should be made to carry all the skis of a squad in one bundle. If speed is important and if a sufficient number of hand sleds is available, the skis may also be carried on sleds.

MAINTENANCE OF SKIS AND SLEDS 95

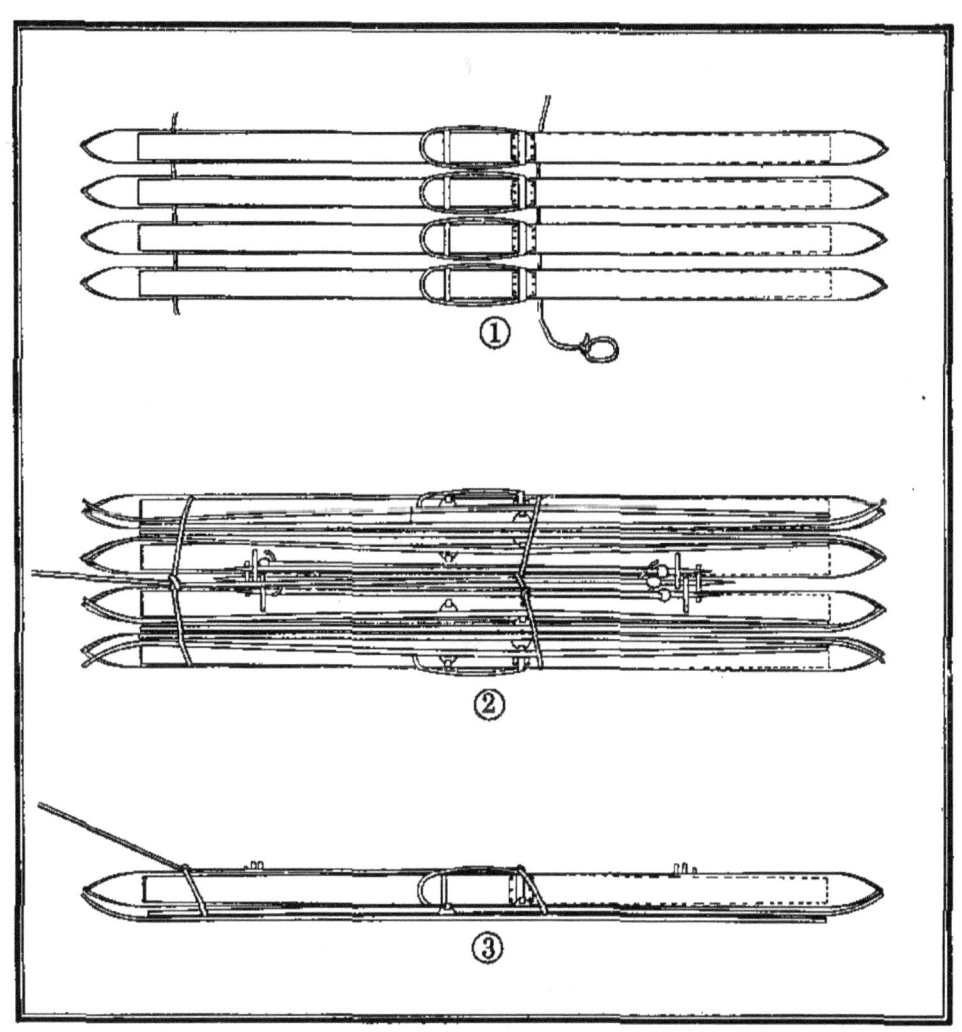

Figure 40.—Sliding ski bundle.

Appendix D. MEANS OF EVACUATING WOUNDED [1]

34. GENERAL

The particularly difficult conditions of winter warfare necessitate special measures for recovering and evacuating the wounded. Good skiers, if available, must be used for this purpose. Instruction in evacuation is an essential part of training in first aid.

By using shelter halves or litters and hand sleds a comparatively fast and safe evacuation is ensured. Whether the first-aid man uses snowshoes or skis depends on the situation, terrain, and snow conditions. If time and circumstances permit, tracks should be prepared or a path trampled in the snow for an evacuation route. Provision should be made for high sleds, or, better yet, akjas, or boat sleds, for transporting wounded men and medical equipment even at the front and during a heavy snowfall.

35. HAND SLEDS AND IMPROVISED MEANS

In some circumstances it may be necessary for two skiers to carry a man between them for short distances. The wounded man is placed on a shelter half, oblique to the direction of travel. The two bearers grasp the shelter half at either end and carry the wounded man between them, leaving their outside arm free for the ski pole. The bearers change places when their "carrying arms" get tired. This method is comparatively comfortable and safe for the wounded man (fig. 41 ①).

If only one bearer equipped with skis is available, the casualty is secured in the same manner. The skier pulls the wounded man by means of a rope fastened to the point of the akja, or boat sled. (See fig. 41 ②.)

---

[1] See also "German Winter Warfare," *Special Series*, No. 18 (15 Dec 1943), sec. XII, p. 149.—EDITOR.

MEANS OF EVACUATING WOUNDED 97

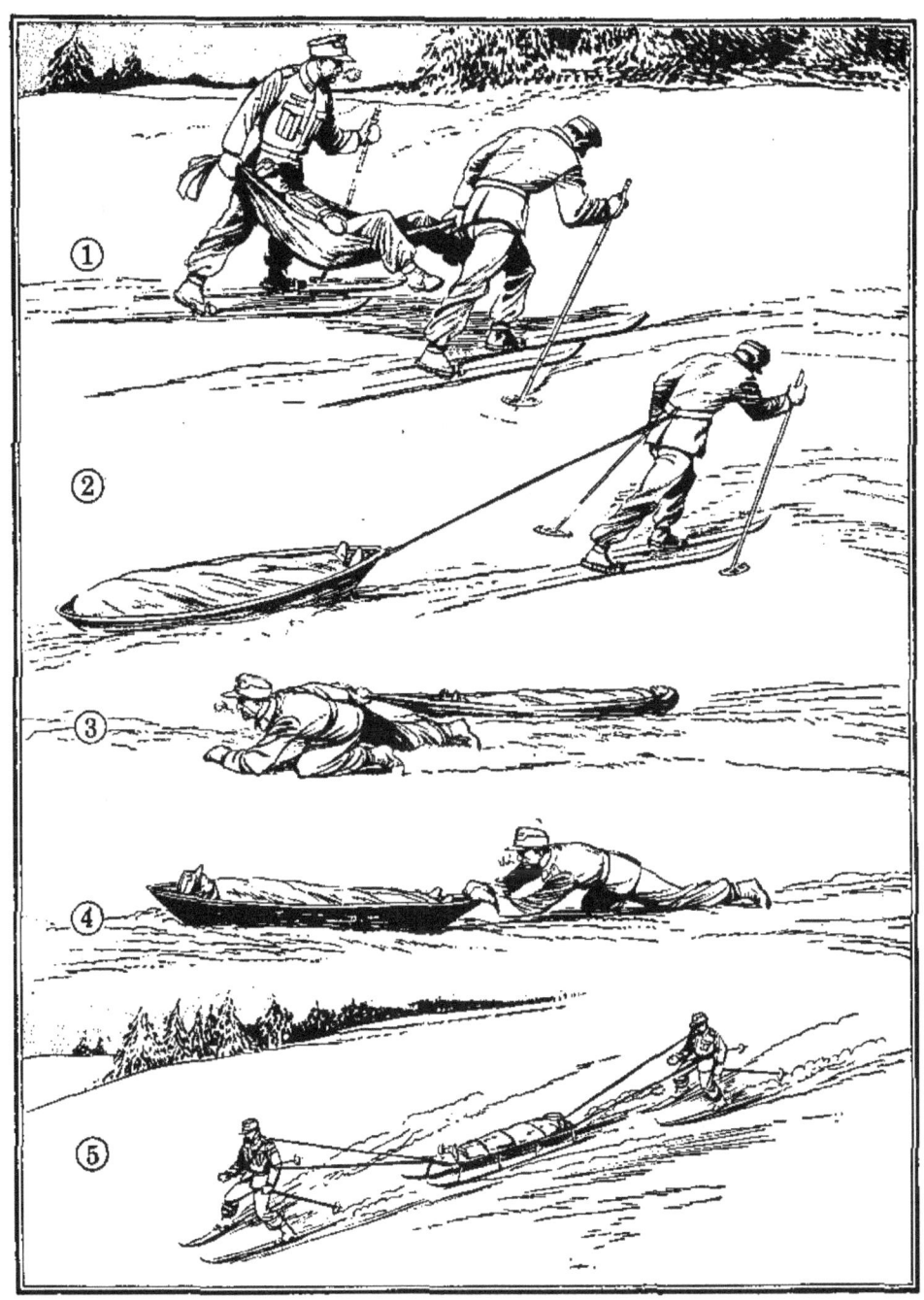

Figure 41.—Methods of evacuating the wounded.

A wounded man may be wrapped in a shelter half, secured with straps and belts, and dragged like a bundle. (See fig. 41 ③.) This method may be useful for evacuating a casualty from a field of fire to a defiladed area.

Akjas, or boat sleds, are used in terrain under enemy observation or under direct fire. The wounded man is tied to the sled (which has been padded with woolen or fur blankets) with ropes or straps, and is pulled or pushed by the bearer. (See fig. 41 ④.)

In easy terrain and under favorable conditions of snow one skier is sufficient to haul a sled, but, as a rule, two men are employed to negotiate obstacles and slopes and to make greater speed. (See fig. 41 ⑤.)

The fireman's carry [2] may be used if only one bearer is available to carry a wounded man (fig. 42). The bearer keeps his ski poles in his right hand, using them to keep his balance.

---

[2] This is the familiar fireman's carry prescribed in FM 21-11, *First Aid for Soldiers* (7 Apr 1943), except that in the German illustration the wounded man's head is over the carrier's right shoulder instead of over the left shoulder.—EDITOR.

Figure 42.—Fireman's carry

Appendix E. IDENTIFICATION

36. INDIVIDUAL AND UNIT IDENTIFICATION

a. Brassards

Winter conditions often make it very hard to distinguish between friend and foe even at short distances. Therefore, the use of certain distinguishing marks is necessary, and the troops must be advised in orders of their meaning. For individual identification, brassards in two colors (black and red), about 3 inches wide, are worn. They can be buttoned on either the right or the left sleeve. To avoid imitation by the enemy, they can be changed periodically, just like passwords. Eight different ways of wearing the brassards are possible, as follows:

(1) Black brassard on left upper arm.
(2) Black brassard on right upper arm.
(3) Black brassard on both upper arms.
(4) Red brassard on left upper arm.
(5) Red brassard on right upper arm.
(6) Red brassard on both upper arms.
(7) Black brassard on left upper arm and red brassard on right upper arm.
(8) Black brassard on right upper arm and red brassard on left upper arm.

b. Manner of Wearing Belt

The manner of wearing the belt depends on the style used by the enemy, and should be changed accordingly. If, for example, the enemy does not wear belts, German troops should wear belts over the outer clothing. Another method of identification is to wear a certain number of cartridge pouches, or to wear the bread bag[2] in a certain manner. The prescribed method should be announced in each new tactical order.

---

[1] See also "German Winter Warfare," *Special Series*, No. 18 (15 Dec 1943), sec. VIII, p. 115.—EDITOR.

[2] Similar to the U. S. field bag (musette bag).—EDITOR.

IDENTIFICATION

c. Ground Flags and Signals

The flag is spread out on the snow to identify the unit as a friendly one. It is especially important to know the use of ground panels for communication purposes between ground units and air units. In improvising flags, only dark conspicuous colors should be used (red, black, blue, green). As an anxiliary means of air-ground identification, a swastika pattern may be trampled in the snow, or snow may be shoveled away to expose the soil in a swastika pattern.

Ski poles and rifles may be used as follows as a means of identification: raise the right or left ski pole up to shoulder height; move a ski pole in circles over the head, in front or to one side; carry the rifle slung over the right or left shoulder, or around the neck. Since these methods of identification can easily be imitated by the enemy, daily changes are necessary.

d. Passwords and Blinker Signals

Familiar names should be used as passwords. (Example: challenge, "Garmisch"; countersign, "Partenkirchen."[3]) This method of identification may be used by day as well as by night and can be imitated by the enemy only with difficulty. It is advisable to choose as passwords the names of rivers, towns, or mountains from the home region of the unit.

Blinker signals with flashlights are to be used primarily in darkness or fog. The sequence of colors must be prearranged. For example, the reply to a challenge given with a red blinker signal should be made with a green one.

---

[3] Garmich-Partenkirchen are twin towns in Bavaria, and are usually mentioned together.—EDITOR.

www.ingramcontent.com/pod-product-compliance
Lightning Source LLC
Chambersburg PA
CBHW080518110426
42742CB00017B/3164